690
on

D1239526

The Pursuit of the Holy

Conquest and Fulfillment of Attainable Levels in Christian Living

by

J. OSWALD SANDERS

Chan King Yin

18th Aug., 1979.

ZONDERVAN PUBLISHING HOUSE
A DIVISION OF THE ZONDERVAN CORPORATION
GRAND RAPIDS, MICHIGAN

THE PURSUIT OF THE HOLY
© 1972 by Zondervan Publishing House
Grand Rapids, Michigan

Second printing   June 1972
Third printing   February 1973

Library of Congress Catalog Card Number 73-171199

All rights reserved

No portion of this book may be reproduced in any form
without the written permission of the publishers, with the
exception of brief excerpts quoted in magazine reviews, etc.

An enlarged and revised edition of
Christ Indwelling and Enthroned

PRINTED IN THE UNITED STATES OF AMERICA

CONTENTS

Preface

PREFACE

The Scriptures present the Christian life as one in which the legitimate aspirations of the heart find their fulfillment in Christ, a life characterized by conquest, not defeat.

The unrelated and yet complementary addresses which compose this volume were delivered at conventions after the "Keswick" pattern in different countries around the world. Their aim is wholly practical. In conventions of this sort the object in view is not the mere impartation of Biblical truth, but to accompany it with such pointed application and appeal as would encourage hearers to put the teaching to the test and take new steps of faith. This accounts for the form in which the addresses appear.

In the first section the messages aim at diagnosing maladies of the spiritual life which beset so many Christians in these confusing times, and indicating what appears to be the Scriptural prescription for the disorder. The second section is a connected series of Bible studies in which the spiritually instructive trek of the Israelites from the banks of the River Jordan to the Promised Land is used, as did St. Paul, to draw contemporary and relevant spiritual lessons.

The fact that, in their spoken form, the Lord has been pleased to bless these messages to Christians of many nationalities has encouraged me to issue this new revised and enlarged edition.

J. OSWALD SANDERS

Auckland, New Zealand

Part One

THE FULFILLED LIFE

A series of conference addresses aimed at diagnosing common maladies of the Christian life and suggesting the biblical prescription.

THE SACRED FIRE

Jesus, Thine all-victorious love
 Shed in my soul abroad;
Then shall my feet no longer rove,
 Rooted and fixed in God.

Oh, that in me the sacred fire
 Might now begin to glow,
Burn up the dross of base desire
 And make the mountains flow.

Thou, who at Pentecost didst fall,
 Do Thou my sins consume,
Come, Holy Ghost, for Thee I call,
 Spirit of burning, come!

Refining fire, go through my heart,
 Illuminate my soul;
Scatter Thy life through every part
 And sanctify the whole.

My stedfast soul from falling free
 Shall then no longer move,
While Christ is all the world to me,
 And all my heart is love.

Charles Wesley

1 THREE PLANES OF SPIRITUAL LIFE

> But the *natural* man receiveth not the things of the Spirit of God: for they are foolishness unto him: neither can he know them, because they are spiritually discerned. 1 Corinthians 2:14
>
> And I, brethren, could not speak unto you as unto spiritual, but as unto *carnal*, even as unto babes in Christ. I have fed you with milk, and not with meat: for hitherto ye were not able to bear it, neither yet now are ye able. For ye are yet carnal: for whereas there is among you envying, and strife, and divisions, are ye not carnal, and walk as men? For while one saith, I am of Paul; and another, I am of Apollos; are ye not carnal? 1 Corinthians 3:1-4
>
> But he that is *spiritual* judgeth all things, yet he himself is judged of no man. 1 Corinthians 2:15

CLASS AND CASTE have characterized and divided human society from time immemorial. Between the clearly defined classes have grown up almost insuperable barriers. The workingman would find himself ill-at-ease among the socialites of a community, and the socialite would be equally at a loss in the home of a craftsman.

In the spiritual realm, an equally clear cleavage exists, but it differs from usually accepted classifications. In the New Testament the apostle Paul, guided by the Inspiring Spirit, divides mankind into three categories. These are not determined by considerations of social status, intellectual attainments, or inherent goodness or badness. The determining factor is the ability of the respective groups to receive and understand and react to spiritual truth.

The Word of God is the touchstone, and the reaction of a man to its truths automatically places him in one of the three categories specified by Paul in the passages at the head of this chapter.

9

THE NATURAL MAN

Of the first category of men, Paul uses the word *psuchikos,* the man of nature. It includes in its scope all those who, however attractive and estimable they may be in all other respects, are unregenerate and whose spirits are, therefore, void of the Spirit of God.

That the natural man labors under a twofold disqualification in matters of the spirit is clear from Paul's description. "The natural man *receiveth not* the things of the Spirit of God: for they are foolishness unto him: *neither can he know them,* because they are spiritually discerned."

First, he *lacks the taste* for spiritual things; he does not appreciate them "because they are foolishness"—meaningless—"to him."

A lover of art will stand transfixed before a masterpiece of Raphael or Turner, oblivious of the passage of time. An uneducated youth with no taste for the refinements of art would pass them by without a second glance. He can see nothing in them, for there is nothing in him to which they would appeal.

The same youth, however, may be seen a few minutes later outside a theater, fascinated and charmed by the hideous, salacious movie posters. He does not receive the things of beauty and art; they are foolishness to him. His tastes lie in a different direction.

The natural man is just as unappreciative of those things which constitute the charm and beauty of the spiritual life. He can appreciate ordinary or even classical literature, but fails to perceive in the Bible that which is more necessary and more to be desired than daily food. He has no appreciation for and sees no value in spiritual truth; it is foolishness to him.

Second, *he lacks the faculty* by which spiritual truth is comprehended. *"Neither can he know them,* because they are spiritually discerned."* He can no more know the things of the Spirit of God than can an unborn babe know the things of terrestrial life. "Except a man

10

be born again, he *cannot* see [or understand] the king-dom of God" (John 3:3).

A man born deaf is unmoved by the most exquisite symphony; a man born blind perceives no beauty in the most glorious sunset. Both these men lack the faculties by which these pleasures may be appreciated.

The natural man is similarly handicapped in the things of the Spirit. He can understand the words of Scripture in their grammatical and etymological sense; he can grasp the geography, history, and ethical teach-ing of the Scriptures; but he can never understand or communicate to others their spiritual content. For this reason an unlettered but spiritual Christian may be a more reliable guide in spiritual things than a brilliant but unregenerate theological professor. Education alone is an inadequate qualification for the ministry of the Word.

William Wilberforce, emancipator of the slaves, was an earnest Christian. He was deeply interested in the spiritual welfare of William Pitt, the brilliant young man who was Prime Minister of Britain at the age of twenty-five. On one occasion Wilberforce persuaded Pitt to attend a drawing-room meeting at which Lord Robert Cecil was the speaker; he fervently hoped that the meeting would result in Pitt's conversion.

Recounting the incident later, Wilberforce said that he had never heard Lord Cecil preach with more power, logic, and unction. He did not see how Pitt could fail to be moved.

As they left the gathering, Wilberforce asked, "Well, what did you think of Cecil's message?" Pitt was silent for a moment, and then he replied, "To tell you the truth, I gave Cecil my whole attention, but I was utter-ly unable to follow what he was driving at?" Sincere, brilliant, Pitt still lacked the faculty by which spiritual truth is apprehended.

Included in the category of the natural man may be those who are cultured, refined, intellectual, even out-

11

wardly religious, as well as those who are drunken, debauched, illiterate, and godless. Indeed, it is to the former class that Paul is primarily referring in this passage. Despite the wide divergence in qualities, both groups suffer from the same fatal disqualification — a lack of taste and a lack of the faculty to know the things of the Spirit of God. Both are equally unable to receive and know spiritual truth.

To use Old Testament symbolism—and for this we have New Testament warrant in First Corinthians 10:11—the natural man *lives in Egypt,* the world, under the bondage of Pharaoh, the devil. He works laboriously under the taskmaster, sin, and for all his work receives only the lash. His great need is to get out of Egypt and from under the power and relentless bondage of his cruel master.

THE CARNAL MAN

The word Paul uses to describe those in the second category is *sarchikos,* the man of the flesh, who "walks on the purely human level of his lower nature." "And I, brethren, could not speak unto you as unto spiritual, but as unto *carnal,* even as unto babes in Christ." It should be stated here that the word does not imply carnality necessarily, in the ordinary sense of indulgence in sexual sin. The sense is rather that he is under the domination of his unregenerate nature.

By his faith this man is united to Christ, but he does not find his full satisfaction in Christ alone. It must always be Christ plus someone else or something else. He is not really joyous, for his happiness is fitful, but he is leagues ahead of the natural man because, unlike the latter, he possesses spiritual life.

His characteristics are clearly delineated in our scripture passage:

Spiritual Infancy — 1 Corinthians 3:1

"He is a babe." The carnal Christian is a believer who, by reason of his age in the faith, should be eating

12

solid food instead of remaining an anemic, milk-drinking spiritual infant. . He is a spiritual dwarf who has never attained full maturity. If after an absence of ten years you converse with him on spiritual themes, you will find he has made little progress, still using the same sterile phraseology, whether in testimony or in prayer— if indeed he does pray and testify. Baby talk is charming, but what is charming in a child is tragic in a man.

He is helpless and *dependent on others* for his spiritual sustenance. He must constantly have someone attend to him in his troubles. Consequent on his own helplessness, he is powerless to help others. He is so occupied with his own pleasures and sorrows that he forgets the duty devolving on him as his brother's keeper.

Like a baby, he tends to be *touchy and quarrelsome over trifles*. He is usually the storm center in the church. The deeper truths of Scripture do not interest him greatly, but he will always be ready to quibble over nonessentials or fight for matters of secondary importance.

He lives in the realm of his emotions and is guided by his feelings rather than by principle. Consequently he is easily offended and not easily pacified. Those who work with him have to walk carefully lest they offend his delicate sensibilities.

He suffers from a *feeble digestion*. When he should, by reason of age and experience, be feeding others with the solid food of the Word, he himself must be bottle-fed with milk. Milk is simply solid food that has passed through the digestion of another. The carnal Christian has a poor appetite for the Bible and is dependent on human teachers for his spiritual sustenance. He is quite incapable of drawing adequate soul-food from the pages of Scripture. Another must do this for him, but he will complain when the preacher gives solid food and not merely milk. When deprived

13

of Christian fellowship, he has no inner spiritual resources and wilts or drifts back into the old life.

Sectarianism — 1 Corinthians 3:4

The carnal Christian tends to laud and follow human leaders and easily falls into narrow sectarianism. "One saith, I am of Paul; and another, I am of Apollos; are ye not carnal?"

Sectarian talk is baby talk, as is the excessive adulation of human leaders in the church. While we should be loyal to the tenets of the denomination with which God has led us to associate, the closer we walk with our Lord, the broader will be our spiritual sympathies. True spirituality always broadens our fellowship and leads us to the recognition of the true oneness in Christ of all believers.

The carnal Christian will often be fiercely loyal to his own particular group and will endeavor to stifle missionary or evangelistic initiative in the church if it does not center in "our denomination."

Contentiousness — 1 Corinthians 3:3

"There is among you envying, and strife, and divisions, are ye not carnal?" These are the natural issue of the carnal state. The carnal believer will form parties and cliques within the church to further his views, and may even adopt questionable methods in ecclesiastical politics to attain his ends. How often are worldly people staggered at what can take place behind the walls of a church! These are not the activities of a spiritual man. The carnal Christian cannot rejoice in the success of a rival, nor can he bear to see another advanced or preferred before him.

Spiritual Defeat

He is often under the heel of sin. "I am carnal, sold under sin," wrote Paul. "For what I would, that do I not; but what I hate, that do I" (Rom. 7:14, 15). Temper, lust, jealousy, pride, and uncharitableness in-

14

vade his heart and find him an easy prey. He fails constantly in his prayer life, and the victories he does gain over temptation are evanescent.

Worldliness — 1 Corinthians 3:3

The carnal man walks, in the main, on the same plane as the natural man. "Are ye not carnal, and walk as [ordinary] men?"

He is frequently dominated by the same desires, governed by the same standards, and actuated by the same motives as the man of the world. There is little appreciable difference between his life and that of a man of the world. His heart has never really broken from its love of the world. While professing to be married to Christ (Rom. 7:4), he lives a life of infidelity, flirting with one of the chief enemies of his Beloved, forgetting that "the friendship of the world is enmity with God" (James 4:4). Although the carnal man is truly a Christian, because some or all of the above characteristics are present in his life, he is constantly grieving or quenching the Holy Spirit, with the result that He is not able to exercise His power on his behalf.

To revert again to Old Testament symbolism, the carnal Christian *lives in the wilderness,* the barren desert lying between Egypt and Canaan, in which territory he is able to enjoy the pleasures of neither. One moment he is on the very borders of the Promised Land, but the next, allured by the memories of the past, he hurries back to the borders of the enemy territory of Egypt. He is constantly torn between the two.

The memory of the onions and the leeks and the garlic of Egypt lingers nostalgically in his mind and renders him strangely reluctant to sample the grapes and milk and honey of Canaan. At special meetings he longs for the victory of Canaan, but when he returns to the old scene, he cannot resist the subtle lure of Egypt. And when no one is looking, he may make a surreptitious excursion back into the forbidden territory. There are no satisfied Christians in the wilderness.

THE SPIRITUAL MAN

The word *pneumatikos* is used by Paul to describe the spiritual man, the man whose life is controlled by the Holy Spirit. He is not only united to Christ but is fully satisfied with Him. Because he is rightly related to the Holy Spirit and obedient to His promptings, the ungrieved Spirit is able to move and work through him in a way impossible with the carnal man.

Unhindered by carnality, He is able to reproduce in him the holy character of Christ, empower him for service, and impart consistent victory over temptation and sin.

The spiritual man is characterized by:

Maturity — Hebrews 5:14

"But strong meat belongeth to *them that are of full age*" — *mature,* runs the passage. The spiritual man is no babe with bottle and comforter. He has the taste for solid food. Although welcoming all that he can learn from gifted human teachers, he is no longer entirely dependent on them for his spiritual rations.

Realizing that the Church includes believers of every nation and denomination, he ceases to be racially exclusive or strongly sectarian. His interests are global, for "the field is the world."

While not of a contentious disposition, he will, if convictions demand, "contend earnestly for the faith."

His Christian life is dynamic, not static. He has left behind the ABC of the doctrine of Christ and continues to progress toward full maturity (Heb. 6:1). More and more territory is daily brought under the sway of his Master.

Discernment — 1 Corinthians 2:15

The spiritual man does not fall prey to erroneous teaching, for "he that is spiritual judgeth (discerneth)

16

all things." The ungrieved Spirit of truth within fore-warns him of the approach of the spirit of error. His scent is keen for error in book or sermon, but while he is discerning, he is not critical or censorious in spirit. His knowledge in the things of the Spirit may be more intuitive than reasoned, but he discerns all things.

Ability to teach — Hebrews 5:12

The spiritual man, no longer preoccupied with his own spiritual state, is able to pass on to others the spiritual teaching he himself has received. He does not come under the stricture, "For when for the time ye ought to be teachers, ye have need that one teach you again which be the first principles of the oracles of God." Instead, he is skillful in the Word of righteousness. It is not necessarily implied that the public teaching of the Word of God is in view here, but it does imply that he is one who can impart spiritual truth to others, whether in public or in private.

Other-worldliness — 1 Corinthians 3:3

He does not "walk as [ordinary] men." His manner of life is fundamentally and radically different from that of the ordinary man or even from that of the carnal Christian. He lives on an entirely different plane of spiritual life. He experiences "life on the highest plane," "life more abundant." The world is powerless to lure him away from Christ, in whom he finds endless joy and satisfaction. He is in the grip of "the powers of the world to come."

An Enigma — 1 Corinthians 2:15

Both the natural man and the carnal are utterly at a loss to understand the spiritual man. "He himself is judged [discerned] of no man." The world can understand neither his tastes nor his outlook. He is perennially joyous, even in the midst of devastating reverses, and for this the world can find no satisfactory explanation.

17

Because he is controlled by the Holy Spirit, he bears the fruit of the Spirit in his character and manifests the power of the Spirit in fruitful service. When the Master comes to his tree, He finds not only leaves, but luscious fruit.

Using Old Testament symbolism, the spiritual man *lives in Canaan,* the Promised Land. The old, unsatisfying life, both of Egypt and of the wilderness, has been bidden an eternal farewell. Between him and the life of bondage in Egypt lies the Red Sea. Between him and the life of alternating victory and defeat in the wilderness roll the waters of Jordan, the river of death. The old life has now no more appeal for him than it has for a dead man.

Instead, he enjoys a life of liberty and victory under the leadership of the Heavenly Joshua. Under his new Leader's guidance, the walls of the hitherto impregnable Jerichos fall crashing to the ground.

It remains for us to discover to which category we belong, on which spiritual plane we are living—natural, carnal, or spiritual? In which country do we live— Egypt, the Wilderness, or Canaan?

If we are in the first category, never having experienced the new birth, provision has been made for us to leave Egypt and escape from the bondage of Pharaoh through the atonement of Christ, God's Passover Lamb. "But as many as received him, to them gave he power to become the sons of God, even to them that believe on his name" (John 1:12).

If we have come to the place where we have to acknowledge that we are yet carnal, knowing mainly the wilderness life of defeat, there is provision for us to know life more abundant. We can step from the carnal to the spiritual plane of experience.

We do not *grow* out of carnality into spirituality, any more than Israel grew out of the wilderness into Canaan. For them—and for us—it was *a step of faith.*

They stepped out of the wilderness into Canaan, and the transition involved for them:

A confession and consciousness of failure in having disobeyed the Lord in refusing to cross into the Promised Land.

A willingness to obey the will of God, as revealed to them through His servant Joshua, to have done with the old life, and to venture into the new.

A step of faith. With no other warrant than the naked promise of God, the priests had to step into the turbulent waters of the flooded Jordan before there was any display of divine power in the parting of the waters. As they obeyed God's command, they experienced divine cooperation. It remains for us to take the same decisive step as the priests. It will be a step of blind faith, but it will be followed by consciousness of the joyous experience of the Land of Promise.

THE HIDDEN FOE

Oh, I could go through all life's troubles singing,
    Turning earth's night to day
If self were not so fast around me, clinging
    To all I do or say.

My very thoughts are selfish, always building
    Mean castles in the air;
I use my love of others for a gilding
    To make myself look fair.

I fancy all the world engrossed with judging
    My merit or my blame;
Its warmest praise seems an ungracious grudging
    Of praise which I might claim.

In youth or age, by city, wood, or mountain,
    Self is forgotten never;
Where'er we tread, it gushes like a fountain
    And its waters flow for ever.

Alas! no speed in life can snatch us wholly,
    Out of self's hateful sight;
And it keeps step, whene'er we travel slowly
    And sleeps with us at night.

O Lord! that I could waste my life for others,
    With no ends of my own,
That I could pour myself into my brothers,
    And live for them alone.

Such was the life Thou livedst; self-abjuring,
    Thine own pains never easing,
Our burdens bearing, our just doom enduring,
    A life without self-pleasing.

F. W. Faber

2 THE SHADOW OF SELF

> If any man will come after me, let him deny himself,
> and take up his cross, and follow me.   Matthew 16:24

WHEN SCULPTING one of his masterpieces, the peerless
Italian artist Michelangelo always affixed to his cap a
small lamp, lest his own shadow falling on the statue
should cause him to mar its perfection.

> There is a man who often stands
> Between me and Thy glory.
> His name is Self, my carnal Self
> Stands 'twixt me and Thy glory.
>   O mortify him, mortify him!
>   Put him down, my Saviour!
> Exalt Thyself alone!
> Lift high the banner of the Cross,
> And 'neath its folds
> Conceal the standard-bearer.

Often the shadow of self falling on our best service
for the Master limits its effectiveness and robs Him of
His glory. It will be to our great advantage to discover
the subtleties of the self-life and to unfold the secret
of its practical crucifixion.

It has been rightly claimed that no branch of knowledge has been so neglected as self-knowledge. All other
forms of knowledge are flattering and bring glory to
their possessors, but this, if we are ruthlessly honest,
is humbling to the extreme. "In me, that is in my
flesh [self], dwelleth no good thing," confessed Paul.

It is no easy task to explore honestly this neglected
branch of knowledge, and it cannot be achieved apart
from the aid of the searchlight of God's Spirit and
God's Word. Self is not likely to reveal its own ugliness.

"There is no more difficult lesson in the Christian
life than to attain a true knowledge of what self is,"

wrote Andrew Murray. "Its terrible power, its secret and universal rule, and the blinding influence it exerts in keeping us from the knowledge of what it is." Let us seek the aid of the Holy Spirit as we embark on a voyage of self-discovery.

What Is Self?

In Bible language, self is "the flesh"; "I"; "the carnal mind." It is the whole life of nature, whether good or bad, all that we received through natural birth. The self-life is the inveterate and implacable foe of the Christ-life in the believer, for the sensual nature passionately resists the Spirit, as does the Spirit the sensual nature: "these are antagonistic to each other" (Gal. 5:17, Weymouth). William Law called self "the devil's peculiar workshop, the citadel of Satan in the soul."

In the heart of the believer, self occupies the same relation to Satan as does the Holy Spirit to Christ. Even after many gross forms of evil have been evicted, self remains to contest and usurp the claim of Christ to the throne of the redeemed life. Self is guilty of treason against the King of Kings and is, therefore, worthy of death.

The subtlety of the self-life lies in that it so successfully blinds us to its own true nature. While its workings are painfully evident to the observer, the victim may be quite unconscious of its hateful presence. But poison is never more dangerous than when its presence is invisible in the sparkling water. In its every form and manifestation, whether in the outburst of sensuality or the garb of religious observance, the self-life stands condemned, for "they that are in the flesh"—dominated by the self-life—"cannot please God."

How Is Self Manifested?

> "How many subtle forms it takes
>   Of seeming verity . . ."

Self can remain concealed under many forms of goodness and, chameleonlike, can adapt itself to any

22

surroundings. It can pray and preach like an angel; it can be gracious and generous. But it mars and spoils all it touches.

The key test of the self-life is this: it is seen in every disposition or temper which is the opposite of that manifested in Christ when He was on earth. It is the difference between "the carnal mind" and "the mind of Christ."

Just as a beam of light falling on a prism is immediately split up into the primary colors, so the self-life, seen in the light of the pure and holy life of Christ, is resolved into its many repulsive manifestations. We shall contrast these with "the mind which was in Christ Jesus," for our sense of need will be in proportion to our knowledge of self.

Self-will

The first manifestation, both in order and in importance, is self-will, the disposition to have our own way. "We have turned every one to his own way." Parents know how early it develops in children. Catherine Booth maintained that her decisive battle with her son, the late General Bramwell Booth of the Salvation Army, occurred when he was six weeks old. A sweet little girl said to her father, "Daddy, I do like to do what I do like to do."

Self will brook no authority other than its own and is determined to have its own way, even if it disobeys God and defies man, hurts others and harms itself. Its watchword is "I will!"

How different it was with the Son of God, whose watchword was, "I seek *not* my own will" (John 5:30, RSV).

Self-seeking

Self eagerly seeks admiration and adulation. It exists for its own pleasure, pride, and glory. It will go to any lengths to achieve prominence or power. It loves to be the center of attraction. It eagerly embraces anything that will advance its interests or oust its rivals. It delights to parade its own attainments. Even the fullness of the Spirit is sought from motives of ambition and aggrandizement, although perhaps not consciously so. It constantly "seeks great things for itself."

How different it was with the Son of God, whose consistent attitude was, "I seek *not* mine own glory" (John 8:50).

Self-assertion

The most hard-worked word in self's vocabulary is the first person personal pronoun singular. Self mistakenly believes that others are as interested in him and his achievements as he himself is. There is no voice he delights to hear as well as his own, so he tends to monopolize the conversation and listens to others only in order to outshine them. He can always tells a better story, recount a worse illness, or prescribe a superior remedy. Try as you may to turn the conversation, it will as inevitably return to the all-absorbing theme as the magnetic needle to its pole. There is a bird, known as the me-bird, which belongs to the same genus as self. It derives its name from the fact that it has only one note, "Me-me, Me-me."

How different it was with our Lord, who claimed, "I am meek and lowly in heart" (Matt. 11:29).

Self-indulgence

Self is motivated by desire, not principle. To want a thing is to have it. It must have its desires gratified in everything, and just when it wants it, too. There is no room for denial or discipline in the philosophy of the self-life. In common with the beasts, it eats and drinks because it likes to eat and drink. It will consent to be enslaved by any fleshly or mental appetite which affords pleasure, whether it be sinful or not. Even legitimate appetites are indulged to such a degree that they become tyrannical.

How different it was with the One who never did

things merely because they pleased Him, but could claim, "I do *always* those things that please him [my Father]" (John 8:29).

Self-pity

Self loves to excite pity and draw out sympathy. It frequently complains about the circumstances or relationships of life and is perpetually and vocally sorry for itself. It exaggerates its sorrows, sufferings, and petty discomforts in its endeavor to induce others to share the burden of its hard lot. The poor tradesman must listen restively to the tale of woe, or he will lose his customer.

The Son of God was not immune to this temptation. On one occasion Peter, with the best of intentions, said to Him, "Pity thyself, Lord." His well-meant exhortation drew from the Master the strong words, "Get thee behind me, Satan; thou savorest not the things that be of God." Jesus knew that self-pity was of Satanic origin. Again, when the women were weeping their way up Calvary, He restrained them with, "Weep not for me"(Luke 23:28).

Self-consciousness

There is a self-consciousness that is part of our human nature and is, therefore, legitimate. But there is a self-consciousness that springs from pride.

Self can never forget itself for a moment. It constantly studies the effect it is producing. It endures agonies if the wrong effect is produced. "Wherever the old man goes, he casts a shadow of himself before. He is constantly occupied with photographing himself and developing the plates." He is easily wounded, imagining slights when none are intended, and is equally difficult to reconcile. Self is often "dissolved in tears, shrouded in silence, or enjoying a pout."

Christ too was self-conscious, but what a difference! "Jesus knowing that . . . he was come from God, and went to God . . . riseth from supper, and laid aside his

garments; and took a towel, and girded himself . . . .
and began to wash the disciples' feet . . ." (John 13:
3-5). His self-consciousness manifested itself in self-
forgetfulness.

Self-depreciation

On occasion self finds it more convenient to magnify
its own inability, especially when some unwelcome or
hidden work that involves self-denial is offering. "Others are much better fitted for the task." But the hollow-
ness of the pretense is soon apparent if someone else
appraises self at its own valuation.

"Well, I thank God I am not proud," said a man to
his friend.

"Neither would I be proud if I were in your place,"
was the rejoinder, "for you have nothing to be proud
about."

"Haven't I?" was the indignant and revealing retort.
"I have as much to be proud about as you have." Such
is self—yours and mine.

In the life of Christ, no such problem arose, for He
was always able to say, "I do always those things that
please him [my Father]" (John 8:29).

Self-love

The soul can have only one supreme object of love
— Christ, self, or some other creature. Self finds its
supreme object of affection in itself. Deny it approba-
tion and praise, and life becomes intolerable. The
motive for Christian service is gone. Self loves others,
not for the pleasure it can bring them, but for the contribution they can make to its own happiness and comfort.

Self performs acts of service and looks back with
"justifiable pride" on the able manner in which it has
been executed. It eagerly endeavors to ascertain what
onlookers thought of the effort. It is for this reason
that God sometimes is compelled to withhold blessing.
To grant it would only feed human pride.

How different it was with the Son of God. Paul spoke of "the Son of God, who loved *me*"—not Himself—"and gave himself for *me*" (Gal. 2:20).

Self-exaltation

As soon as Philip had led the Ethiopian eunuch into the knowledge of Christ, he immediately effaced himself. The six-winged seraphim used two wings to veil their beauty and two to hide their service. But self dwells with smug self-complacency on its achievements, to which it draws the attention of others. Self can preach a sermon, make an appeal, sing a solo, win a soul to Christ, and then go home to congratulate itself on its performance.

How different it was with the Master, who "humbled himself and . . . made himself of no reputation" (Phil. 2:7, 8).

Self-justification

Self always hates to be put in the wrong. Indeed, it is almost impossible to prove self to have been in the wrong. That is why self is rarely willing to apologize. The apology should come from the other person.

Self is always ready with a plausible reason for neglect or failure and is amazingly versatile in vindicating itself and justifying its actions. It is punctilious in exacting its rights and is perennially busy avenging its wrongs.

Although our Lord had the perfect answer for every accusation leveled against Him, we read that "He opened not his mouth," but was "as a sheep before her shearers, dumb." No word of self-justification passed His lips. It is well for us that it was so, for had He justified Himself, He would not have been able to justify us.

Self-confidence

Like Peter, self is confident of its own unaided ability and good judgment. Whatever may happen to others, it will not fall out of the race. "Though all men forsake thee, yet will not I," boasted Peter. Self feels no need of someone wiser or more experienced, for it is satisfied with itself. To self, our Lord's words, "without me ye can do *nothing*," are just poetic license and hardly the exact truth.

And yet the omnipotent Son of God said without any qualification, "I can of mine own self do *nothing*" (John 5:30).

This list of the manifestations of the self-life could be extended considerably, but perhaps enough has been written to unveil some of its subtleties and hatefulness.

It is unlikely that this unretouched portrait of your self and mine will meet with enthusiastic approval, and yet are there not striking resemblances to our baser self? Does it not afford humiliating glimpses of our self? Is it any wonder that it is represented in Scripture as being so abhorrent to God that He nailed it to the cross of His Son? "This we know—that our old self was nailed to the cross with him" (Rom. 6:6, Weymouth).

How Can the Self-life Be Terminated?

There can be no compromise; it *must be* terminated. Like King Agag, it will plead eloquently for its life, saying, "Surely the bitterness of death is past!" But it must not be so. "Saul" — the man dominated by his self-life—"spared Agag," to the loss of his kingdom and, later, his very life, for he was slain by an Agagite. But "Samuel," the man of God, "hewed Agag in pieces."

Theodore Monod in his poem, "The Altered Motto," represents self as offering to compromise:

"And my wistful heart said faintly,
    Some of self, and some of thee."
It might under pressure concede even more:
    "Less of self, and more of thee."

But this cannot be. Christ will brook no rival. Self

28

would be willing to concede to Christ the status of constitutional monarch so long as it could be prime minister, but this is not acceptable to Christ. There is only one acceptable response:

"Higher than the highest heavens,
    Deeper than the deepest sea,
Lord, thy love at last hath conquered;
    Grant me now my soul's desire—
None of self, and all of thee."

If we believed the words of our Lord, we would be convinced that the death of self would be the means of untold spiritual enrichment.

J. Gregory Mantle recounts that when Mahmoud, with his all-victorious armies, laid siege to Guzurat in India, he forced his way into the costliest shrine of the Brahmins. They prostrated themselves before him, offering vast ransom if only he would spare their god, for, they claimed, the fortunes of their city depended on him.

After a pause, Mahmoud replied that he would rather be known as the breaker than the seller of idols, and struck the image with his battle-axe. It proved to be hollow, and had been used as the receptacle for thousands of precious gems, which, as the image was shattered, showered down at the conqueror's feet.

Such an idol is self. To spare the idol would have meant the sacrifice of untold wealth. To spare self means spiritual penury. If we deliver it to utter destruction at the hand of Christ, there will be showered upon us spiritual enrichment beyond our power to conceive.

But how can this tyrant be ousted from the throne it has usurped? We cannot do it ourselves, for self cannot dethrone self. There is a more excellent way which is illustrated in an Old Testament story recounted in 1 Kings 1:5-38.

How was Adonijah, the usurper of the throne rightfully belonging to Solomon, dethroned? By the enthronement of Solomon! The enthronement of Solomon automatically meant the dethronement of Adonijah. So the enthronement of Christ in the heart secures the dethronement of self, for two cannot occupy the throne at the same time.

"Let him deny self," said our Lord, by which He meant, "Let him remove self from the center of authority." The verb is in the aorist tense, implying a crisis. It can take place in a moment of time. It will take place when, by an act of will, we renounce the dominance of self and place Christ on the throne of the heart.

TAKE ME, BREAK ME, MAKE ME

Take me, O Lord, for I am but clay
That lies unused upon a dusty shelf;
I cannot move to meet Thy blessed hand,
So weak am I, and powerless in myself;
I can but cry for Thee with helpless moan,
And ask Thee so to work upon my soul
That I shall let my painful struggles cease,
And yield my hapless life to Thy control.

Break me, O Lord, for hard hath grown the clay,
Until no pliability remains;
Let Thine own fingers crumble me to dust,
Till naught of former shape the clay retains.
The vessel on the wheel was sadly marred,
Some trace of self-life spoiled the Potter's art;
Then sift the scattered dust with searching eye,
And satisfy my broken contrite heart.

Make me, O Lord, with Thine own bleeding hands,
And streams of grace will moisten and unite
The broken dust again to yielding clay,
No more to struggle, and resist Thy might.
Then take, and break, and make, until, so formed,
The Heavenly Potter calls His work complete,
And in His image fair hath fashioned me,
A vessel for the Master's use made meet.

Carrie Judd Montgomery

3 IN THE HAND OF THE POTTER

The word which came to Jeremiah from the Lord, saying, Arise, and go down to the potter's house, and there I will cause thee to hear my words. Then I went down to the potter's house, and, behold, he wrought a work on the wheels. And the vessel that he made of clay was marred in the hand of the potter: so he made it again another vessel, as seemed good to the potter to make it. Then the word of the Lord came to me, saying, O house of Israel, cannot I do with you as this potter? saith the Lord. Behold, as the clay is in the potter's hand, so are ye in mine hand, O house of Israel.

Jeremiah 18:1-6

To the Potter's house I went down one day,
And watched him while moulding a vessel of clay,
And many a wonderful lesson I drew
As I noted the process the clay passed through.
Trampled and broken, downtrodden and rolled,
To render it plastic and fit for the mould.

How like the clay that is human, I thought,
Which in heavenly hands to God's image is brought,
For self must be cast as the dust at His feet
Ere man is renewed, and for service made meet;
And pride must be broken, and self-will lost —
All laid on the altar, whatever the cost;
And all that is boasted of human display
Must yield to God's hand and be taken away.

JEREMIAH THE PATRIOT-PROPHET is deeply distressed. Despite his tears and entreaties his loved nation is pursuing a suicidal course and is drifting farther and farther from God. All his endeavors to avert the impending national disaster have proved unavailing. But in his hour of hopelessness, God grants him a vision of hope—and through a very commonplace scene. "Arise and go down into the potter's house, and there I will cause thee to hear my words," was the divine message.

33

We shall endeavor to reconstruct the circumstances that led to this visit to the potter's house and to learn, as did Jeremiah, the lesson God sought to teach His servant.

This sign of the potter had primary reference to the nation of Israel. Chosen to be a vessel unto honor, through its willfulness and rebellion, Israel had become a marred vessel because they persistently thwarted and resisted the beneficent purpose of the Divine Potter. But even at this late hour came God's symbolic message: If the people will but submit to the touch of the Potter, He will make of them "another vessel," as seems good to Him.

The parable has another and individual application —for a nation is only the aggregation of individuals— from which great encouragement may be drawn. In the potter's house, Jeremiah saw the three things we would see in a potter's workshop today, for there has been singularly little change in the potter's art.

The potter himself, well-versed in his art, with skillful fingers and imaginative mind, is surrounded by vessels of utility and beauty, the work of his own hands. *The wheel*—a round piece of board set horizontally on top of a revolving spindle which moves faster or slower according to the pressure of the potter's foot on the treadle. Then in the potter's hand he sees *the clay,* ordinary material with no inherent beauty, no capacity for self-improvement, but capable of receiving and retaining the design conceived in the potter's mind. So on the wheel and through the medium of the clay, the potter is working into visibility the pattern already conceived in thought.

Obedient to the heavenly command, the prophet stands at the potter's side and watches him at work.

THE PARABLE INTERPRETED

"The potter wrought a work on the wheels" (v. 3).

The craftsman takes a lump of clay, cuts it into small pieces, crushes them together on the bench, cuts and crushes it together again and again, until all bubbles and lumps have been removed. Taking the lump of prepared clay, he throws it into the center of the wheel, so that it sticks fast, revolving with the wheel. As the wheel revolves, his deft fingers shape it, first without and then within until a vessel of beauty emerges from the unpromising clay.

What is the interpretation of the parable?

Who but God can be the counterpart of *the potter?* The prophet Isaiah leaves us in no doubt: "But now, O Lord, thou art our Father; we are the clay, and thou our potter" (Isa. 64:8). And a supremely skillful Potter He is. Moulding lives is not a matter of experiment with Him. There is no caprice in the movements of His hands. He is a vastly experienced Potter who perfects what He begins and does not lightly abandon His purpose.

The figure of *the potter* may seem frightening, for the clay is utterly at the mercy of the potter. But Isaiah assures us that God's sovereignty never clashes with His paternity. He will never exercise His sovereignty in the manner of an eastern despot. He is our Father as well as our Potter, and His sovereign will is never inconsistent with His Fatherhood. The foot that controls the wheel and the hand that moulds the clay are nail-pierced.

Human nature finds it hard to submit to the absolute sovereignty of God, and it has the disastrous tendency of assuming the role of potter. So often we take our lives into our own hands and arrogantly try to mould our own destiny. But this is fatal. We do have the God-like power of free-will, but we realize our true destiny only when we learn that "Our wills are ours . . . . to make them Thine." "We are the clay, and Thou our potter."

And the wheels? It would be difficult to find a more satisfying interpretation of their significance than Browning's oft-quoted lines:

> . . . . this dance
> Of plastic circumstance,
> This present, thou, forsooth, wouldst fain arrest:
> Machinery just meant
> To give thy soul its bent,
> Try thee and turn thee forth, sufficiently impressed.

The daily circumstances of life and all they bring to us constitute the wheel on which our character and personality are being fashioned. All of God's providential dealings with us are devised to perfect His design. Temperament and environment, joy and sorrow, prosperity and adversity, births and bereavements—all these are the wheel which revolves under the control of our Potter's foot. If there were no design behind it all, how could we explain the amazing complexity of life's circumstances?

If it is on the wheel that the design in the potter's mind is transferred to the plastic clay, does this not mean that complaints against our circumstances are in reality directed against the Potter who ordered them? No other circumstances than those in which we find ourselves at this moment could achieve His highest purpose for our lives. Our need is not so much a change of circumstances as a change of attitude toward them.

Life is no blind whirring of wheels, but a wonderful mosaic of circumstances ordered with meticulous care by a loving Father. To rebel against them is only to achieve our own unhappiness and the marring of the vessel of our life.

> 'Tis I who mar His working (that e'er is faultless),
> I am so blind,
> I do not see that many a painful process
> Is love most kind;
> How oft I struggle, chafe at sitting still,
> Marring the working of His blessed will.

And the clay? "Thou hast made me as the clay," said Job (10:9)—a statement which is true both physically and spiritually, for it was of earth that God first formed man. "Man is but a handful of dust along the

36

road of life." Clay — common, unlovely, unclean — is human nature, the raw material for the Kingdom of God.

The value in the perfect vessel lies not in the clay but in the art of the potter. "It is the art which gives the value, not the material," said Dresser. Left to itself, clay would remain clay. Yielded to the shaping hands, there are no limits to its possibilities.

Like clay, a human life has almost infinite possibilities. Geologists affirm that there are endless varieties of clay, each locality having its own particular varieties. no two of which can be treated alike. The Heavenly Potter, knowing that no two of His creatures are the same, does not deal with us *en masse*. He bestows on each individual attention. His dealings are unique and exclusive.

It has been objected that the analogy we are drawing is hardly correct, for the factor of self-determination and self-will does not enter into the relation of potter and clay, as it does into that of God and man.

Dr. G. Campbell Morgan has pointed out that there is in reality a greater gulf between the potter and the clay than there is God and man, for the clay is not in the image of the potter, but man is in the image of God. On the part of the clay, all that is necessary for the achievement of the potter's pattern is *negative acquiescence*. On the part of man, however, the Divine Potter requires much more—*positive cooperation*. Deny Him this, and the vessel is marred. We must be responsive to His slightest touch.

THE PURPOSE CONCEIVED

"As seemed good to the potter" (v. 4).

The conception of life as a vessel is familiar in the Scriptures. Of Paul the Lord said, "He is a chosen vessel unto me, to bear my name . . ." (Acts 9:15). Paul spoke of the possibility of believers being "vessels unto honour, sanctified; and meet for the master's use"

(2 Tim. 2:21). He also said, "But we have this treasure in earthen vessels" (2 Cor. 4:7).

To what end is the Heavenly Potter working? To what use is the vessel He is moulding to be put? To bear His name to the uttermost part of the earth. To display the priceless jewel of Christ's glorious Person and to diffuse His fragrance everywhere. "God . . . through us, spreads the fragrance of the knowledge of Him everywhere, for we are the aroma of Christ to God . . ." (2 Cor. 2:14, 15, RSV).

The clay does not perceive the beautiful design and the beneficent purpose the potter has conceived in his mind, but as it is submissive to his touch, the clay expresses the potter's thought to others. Paul indicates that the very purpose of our creation is to provide God with a medium through which He can make His thought visible and tangible. "We are His handiwork, created in Christ Jesus, to devote ourselves to the good deeds for which God has designed us" (Eph. 2:10, NEB). It is of no importance whether the vessel is used in kitchen or banquet hall, so long as it is "meet for the Master's use."

THE PURPOSE THWARTED

"The vessel that He made of clay was marred in the hand of the potter" (v. 4).

As Jeremiah was admiring the skill of the potter and the vessel which was nearing completion, suddenly a flaw appeared, and the vessel collapsed, a shapeless mass in the potter's hand. Some foreign substance had crept in and thwarted the purpose of the potter. The prophet naturally expected him to throw the marred vessel on the scrap-heap and take up a new lump of clay which would yield to his moulding hands. But to his amazement, the potter took the broken pieces, removed the offending substance, and shaped the old clay into a new vessel.

Marred in the making, but with wondrous patience
Takes He the clay

Into His hands, and fashions slowly
  In His own way.
Just what I was the world can only see —
He looks beyond, and sees what I can be.

The failure could not be attributed to carelessness or clumsiness on the part of the potter. No craftsman willfully spoils his own work. The cause must lie elsewhere. If we have been worsted in the battle of life, if the Divine ideal for our lives has been frustrated, God will not patch up the old marred vessel. The cause of the failure must be discovered and dealt with.

The Divine Potter's design for a life may be thwarted and the vessel marred in many ways:

Resisting the known will of God is one cause. In most lives there is some one point around which the battle rages. With some it is in the realm of the affections; with others it is personal ambition. Some who have designed their own pattern of life, resent the intrusion of a God who is sovereign and requires obedience to His will. The consistency of the clay is so stiff and resistant that it fails to respond to the Potter's touch. To become vessels unto honor and meet for the Master's use, the arms of our rebellion must be laid at His feet.

The secret toleration of sin may be another element in the failure. A vessel that is marred may appear flawless on the exterior, the defect hidden from the eye of all but the Great Potter who was moulding it. It may be a secret sympathy with sin which has not been clearly defined even to one's self, sin cherished in the imagination or in the heart. The harboring of a secret passion will mar the vessel as will an untamed tongue or an uncontrolled temper.

The unwillingness to break with known sin can be the means of marring the vessel—unwillingness to say a decided "No!" to temptation; to make confession to a person we have wronged; to make restitution, financial or otherwise; to forgive one against whom we hold a grudge; to abandon a doubtful practice; to cease robbing God and give Him His tithe—any or all of these are sufficient to thwart the design of the Potter.

Any eccentricity (using the word in its literal sense —a getting off the center of the wheel) will mar the vessel. If it is to be symmetrically shaped, it must be placed *and remain* in the center of the wheel. It is possible for us to have unconsciously shifted from the center of God's will for our lives. It is possible for us to be geographically out of the will of God. If this is so, we must correct our eccentricity.

THE PURPOSE REVISED

> *"The vessel was marred in the hand of the potter . . . . So he made it again, another vessel . . . ."* (v. 4).

Here is the antidote to despair. Though marred, the vessel was still in the hand of the potter. The lesson is clear. No matter how sadly we may have marred our lives or failed to realize our early ideals, if we belong to Christ we are still in the Heavenly Potter's hand, and He does not despair of us. He makes men anew. Jacob the crooked becomes Israel the prince; Peter the denier becomes the Pentecostal preacher; Mark the deserter becomes Mark the profitable. So there are still grounds for hope. The Divine Potter is undiscourageable. We may despair of ourselves, but He never despairs of us.

Years ago Paul Morphy was the world's champion chess player. He was invited by a friend to look at a valuable painting with the caption, "The Chess Player." In it, Satan was represented as playing chess with a young man, the stake being the young man's soul. The game had reached the stage where it was the young man's; but he was checkmated. There was no move he could make which would not mean defeat for him; and the strong feature of the picture was the look of utter despair on his face as he realized that his soul was lost.

Morphy, who knew more about chess than the artist,

studied the picture for a time and then called for a chessboard and men. Placing them in exactly the same position as they were in the painting, he said, "I'll take the young man's place and make the move," and he made the move that would have set the young man free.

Do we, as that despairing young man, feel that we have played and lost in the game of life? Then let us turn over our lives to the One who knows every move of the game, and let Him make us again.

"Another vessel," perhaps not so arresting as the one He originally designed, but yet still "meet for the Master's use." Although through our sin we may not be what we could have been, we need no longer remain what we are. He has another plan that will be to His glory and our blessing. But it must be noted that this new vessel is to be "as seemed good to the potter," not "as seemed good to the clay." The vessel cannot dictate whether it will find its vocation in kitchen or in banquet hall.

In remaking the vessel, the swiftly-moving hands of the potter are not working at random. They are executing an intricate pattern.

On one occasion Dr. W. Morley Punshon, a noted Methodist preacher, visited a pottery in France in company with a lady. The potter was engaged in a piece of beautiful work of such striking and intricate design, that the lady was convinced there must be within his range of vision, some copy from which he was working.

At last Dr. Punshon said to the potter, "The lady wants to know where your pattern is." The man simply pointed to his head. The pattern was in his mind, and as his hands caressed the clay, he was expressing in it, the creation of his mind. The pattern in our Potter's mind may be obscure to us, but it is plain to Him. To faith, this is enough.

The pattern in the Divine Potter's mind has been disclosed to us. "God knew his own before ever they were, and also ordained that they should be shaped to

41

the likeness of his Son" (Rom. 8:29, NEB). Every touch of His hand is working to that end.

The master-mind of Michelangelo saw in a discarded, moss-covered block of marble an angel of transcendent beauty. With His omniscient eye, God discerns in the most unlovely and unpromising life, magnificent possibilities, where others see only failure.

On the whirring wheels of our daily circumstances, God purposes to make of our unpromising lives, a thing of beauty. The touches we so much fear are designed only to remove the ugly things, and to replace shapelessness with symmetry.

THE PURPOSE PERFECTED

"... *as seemed good to the potter to make it*" (v. 4).

> Then, lo! there appeared a most delicate vase
> Of wonderful beauty and exquisite grace;
> Was this the crude clay to the potter once brought?
> And long by his hand in such constancy wrought?
> So fashioned and formed by his marvelous skill
> To a vessel as planned by His marvelous will;
> No longer a trace of the earth or the clay,
> The fires of the furnace had burned them away.

To perfect the vessel, the potter uses not only the wheel but the fire. If the work done on the vessel is to be permanent, if it is to retain the design of the potter, it must pass through the fire. The firing process imparts hardness and strength to the vessel, as well as bringing out the colors that have been painted on it. In the fire the weak vessel is discovered and the unworthy one broken by the heat. It is possible for us to break down at this fire test, and blame the Potter; but we need not flinch as we pass through the furnace. The flames will not kindle on us. He controls the fire as well as the wheel.

It is interesting to note how the vessels are burnt. None is placed in the fire unshielded. It is first encased in some stronger material and carefully sealed. Only then is it placed in the kiln. No Christian is called upon to pass through the fires of affliction alone.

When cast into the fiery furnace, the three Hebrew youths must have been apprehensive. They did not know that under their God's control the flames would burn with strange discrimination, destroying only their confining bonds. They had no expectation of the high honor of the presence of the Son of God with them in the midst of the flames. Yet such was the case.

> When through fiery trials thy pathway shall lie,
> His grace all sufficient shall be thy supply;
> The flame shall not hurt thee, His only design
> Thy dross to consume and thy gold to refine.

When King George V of Britain was paying a visit to a pottery, two special vases were shown to him. Both were made of the same material, and both had been painted in the same style and manner; but one was a beautiful ornament, the other blurred and unsightly. And the reason? One had *taken* the fire and the other had not.

Passing on, the king came to some china which was being made for Buckingham Palace. A young woman was busily engaged painting the inside of the cups black. He could not understand this, for no orders had been placed for black china. He asked to see the special cups that were being prepared for him. Again he was pointed to the same cups. Then the worker explained that beneath the black was gold. When the cup emerged from the fire, the black would be *burnt off* and the gold would be *burnt in*. But if the gold were placed in the fire without the protective black, it would be spoiled. So often we see only the black, and forget that in our Potter's design there is always the gold underneath.

In concluding an address on this subject at the English Keswick Convention, Dr. J. Stuart Holden said, "The last appeal to the marred vessel is the marred Face. He was a marred vessel, marred by sin not His own but yours and mine. And He it is who deals in love and gentleness, and looks upon you, and pleads with you. I pray you, ere we separate, look into the marred Face, and see there the power for the re-making of the marred vessel."

> Remade by Thee, to lie in glad submission
>   Day after day;
> Careful to seek Thy will, Thy plans, Thy guidance,
>   Then to obey;
> Remade, refashioned, grant that all may see
> In time THY wondrous image formed in me.

THE TEMPER OF OUR SOULS

By suffering only can we know
   The nature of the life we live;
The temper of our souls they show,
   How true, how pure, the love we give,
To leave my love in doubt would be
No less disgrace than misery!

I welcome, then, with heart sincere,
   The cross my Saviour bids me take;
No load, no trial is severe
   That's borne or suffered for His sake:
And thus my sorrow shall proclaim
A love that's worthy of the name.

Jeanne Marie de la Motte-Guyon

4 DELIGHTING IN LIFE'S DISCIPLINES

Reading: Hebrews 12:5-13

> Now obviously no "chastening" seems pleasant at the
> time: it is in fact most unpleasant. Yet when it is all over
> we can see that it has quietly produced the fruit of real
> goodness in the characters of those who have accepted
> it in the right spirit.   Hebrews 12:11 (Phillips)

THE PERENNIAL PROBLEM of the sufferings and trials
of the child of God demands a reasonable and satisfying answer, but there is no easy answer to it. While
there may not always be an explanation that immediately satisfies reason, there is always an explanation that
will satisfy faith.

We live in days of mounting world crises and increasingly complex personal and family problems. In
genuine distress of mind, many are asking God, "Why?"
In thus repeating the sin of Eden, they are, unconsciously it may be, depriving themselves of the comfort
and help of the Holy Spirit. It is vitally important to
gain the biblical perspective and adopt the correct attitude toward the disciplines our Heavenly Father ordains. A wrong attitude inevitably means impoverish-
ment in our lives and paralysis in our Christian service.

In the classic passage on this subject, Hebrews 12:
5-13, the key verse is the one at the beginning of this
chapter. It reveals to us:

THE CHARACTER OF LIFE'S DISCIPLINES

These are our kindergarten days—the days of our
"child-training," as the word "chastening" suggests.
Every circumstance of life, whether sad or glad, is
being made tributary to our eternal profit and well-
being by a loving Father. "For our light affliction,

which is but for a moment, worketh for us a far more exceeding and eternal weight of glory" (2 Cor. 4:17). His long-sighted love will not spare us present pain if He sees it is the best way to increase our future joy and blessing.

> We may not see just here and now
> With vision clear the why and how
> Of all that God seems to allow,
>   But "Afterward!"
>
> We may not fully understand
> How underneath God's chastening hand
> Pain is fulfilling love's command,
>   But "Afterward!"

Three fundamental principles of training children have been enunciated:

1. The parent cannot let the child have all his own way; not that he arbitrarily desires to deprive the child of all will, but rather to bring him to choose intelligently and gladly as the parent wisely sees is best for him.

2. The parent, though he may cross the present choice of the child, eagerly yields to any inclination on the child's part towards what the parent shows is best for him. He does not withhold any privilege the child is ready to choose wisely.

3. The great objective of the parent is that the child will one day be free from restraint because his choosing has been so habitually wise as to need no further restriction.

Much light will be thrown upon perplexing experiences in life if we adapt these principles to God's dealings with us. We will come to see that all His chastening and disciplines are designed and conducted in perfect wisdom. All His actions spring from infinite love and can, in consequence, be neither harsh and arbitrary nor unnecessary.

In themselves, there is nothing to the disciplines of life—they are only the means to an end. God does not plough up the soil of our hearts merely to demonstrate

His power and sovereignty. When He sends the plow-share of suffering and trial tearing through us, He has a beneficent objective in view. Samuel Rutherford expressed that purpose in these words:

"Let Him plough—He purposeth a crop."

God's every act of discipline is only the prelude to some act of grace and kindness. His unselfish love will not rest until He has perfected what concerns us and we are "conformed to the image of His Son."

THE CHANNELS OF LIFE'S DISCIPLINES

Chastening may reach us through a variety of channels, but three are prominent:

Our own mistakes and sins. When we see that we have brought our trouble on ourselves, we are more or less resigned to it and accept it. We can see at least some connection between our sin or failure and its outcome, although to our myopic vision the suffering incurred may seem to far outweigh its occasion.

Our watchful Father graciously allows the stroke to fall so that we may search our hearts, discover and confess the sin that induced it, and watch against its recurrence. We will never know, this side of heaven, how often God's chastening hand has saved us from ultimate ruin and eternal loss.

The mistakes and sins of others. Of all life's trials and tests, those most difficult to understand and to accept are those which flood upon us through this channel because not infrequently they seem most unjust and undeserved. This factor has caused many to become "offended in Christ" because they fail to distinguish between what has been termed the *permissive* and the *directive* will of God.

What the other person said or did may have been entirely wrong and unjustifiable. He could not, therefore, have done it at God's *direction,* but God does *permit* men and women to pursue a sinful course they have set their mind upon. When that action reached us, it

49

ceased to be the wrong act of another, so far as we are concerned, and became the permitted will of God for us.

To a Christian walking in fellowship with God, there are no such things as second causes. He shares the Psalmist's assurance that "the steps of a good man are ordered by the Lord." No trial or affliction can reach those who are abiding in Him without His permission. We can be confident in every circumstance of life, however baffling, that it has been permitted in our highest interests by the wisest and most loving of Fathers, who knows exactly how much we can bear, for "God . . . will not suffer you to be tempted above that ye are able [to bear]" (1 Cor. 10:13).

From what we know of God as He has revealed Himself in Jesus Christ, we can accept it as a spiritual axiom that He will not allow one unnecessary stroke to fall, nor will He give us one moment of unnecessary pain. The moment His purpose is achieved, the moment we master the lesson He is teaching us, the chastening ends.

We can safely leave the one who caused our pain in His hands, and we must not endeavor to avenge the wrong. "Vengeance is mine, I will repay" are the Lord's words. If we cherish resentment or a bitter spirit, we will not alleviate our lot, but only retard our own spiritual development and disappoint our heavenly Father.

God's providential dealings. These often seem incomprehensible to us in our hour of distress, and a querulous "Why?" springs unbidden to our lips.

But God is under no obligation to give an explanation of all His actions, nor does He promise to do so. He is not only a loving Father, but also a sovereign God, and it is here that faith finds its opportunity.

> It may not be for me to see
> The meaning and the mystery
> Of all that God has planned for me,
>   But "Afterward!"

After an unparalleled ministry of self-effacement, *John the Baptist* found himself cast into prison. He knew that Jesus, whom he had announced as "the Lamb of God that taketh away the sin of the world," was not far away. Doubtless He would visit the prison to encourage him in his hour of need. But the weeks passed and He did not even send a message of comfort. John's faith began to falter. "Is this really the Messiah? If He were, would He treat me in this way?" he must have wondered.

At last he could bear the disappointment no longer and sent a deputation to Jesus, in the hope that his doubts would be dissolved and his former confidence confirmed. But even to the deputation Jesus gave no direct reply to John's question, "Art thou he that should come, or look we for another?" Instead, Jesus performed miracles that evidenced His Messiahship and told them to tell John what they had seen and to add this message, "Blessed is he, whosoever shall not be offended in Me—who can trust Me, even when cast into prison, who can unquestioningly endure any test to which in My wisdom I subject him."

One visit from Christ would have transformed John's prison into a palace; one word of explanation would have dispelled all his doubts—*but the visit and the word were not forthcoming.* Instead, he was given the infallible and contemporary prescription for joy in the midst of trial: "Happy is he who finds no cause of stumbling in Me."

Lazarus was dying. His devoted sisters sent an urgent message to Jesus: "He whom thou lovest is sick." It never entered their minds that He might not hasten to their side in their distress. But He did not come. "When Jesus heard that Lazarus was sick," the record runs, "he abode two days still in the place where he was." They saw Lazarus' life slowly ebb away, and the ache in their hearts was more acute because their loved Friend had disappointed them.

51

Four days later Jesus arrived, but with no explanation of His delay. Reproachfully the sisters greeted Him, "Lord, if thou hadst been here, our brother had not died." Jesus gave no direct answer, but what He said indicated that He blessed them more by remaining away than by hastening to their side. His meaning became clear afterward, for not only was their brother restored to life, but they came to know Jesus in a new relationship—as the Resurrection and the Life.

In *David's* heart there was a growing passion to do something that would express his love for his God. He would build a house for God so magnificent that it would be worthy of His majesty. "This will I do," said David. But to his disappointment and dismay, his laudable and unselfish plan was met with "Thou shalt not" from God; but the refusal was softened by the word of appreciation, "Nevertheless, it is well that it was in thy heart." It was true then, as now, "What I do, thou knowest not now, but thou shalt know hereafter."

In a hundred ways, through bereavement and sorrow, through pain and suffering, through disappointment and frustration, through physical and mental anguish, through friend and foe, we are tested and tried. How may we find rest of heart and mind in the midst of God's unexplained providences?

The one who finds peace has ceased to ask, "Is God love?" and has substituted, "God *is* love," and the circumstances of life are interpreted in the light of that conviction. He has learned that *in acceptance lies peace*. He has learned to know his God so well that nothing He does, however inscrutable, is misunderstood or shakes his confidence. He has learned that God's richest blessings frequently arrive in packages with a rough exterior.

THE CHALLENGE OF LIFE'S DISCIPLINES

There are three ways in which we may respond to the challenge of the chastening rod, for challenge there

52

is. *We may despise it* (Heb. 12:5) by rebelling instead of submitting, by refusing to learn the obvious lesson; by refusing to acknowledge any reason in ourselves which made the chastening stroke necessary. This attitude leads only to a hardened heart and ultimate loss. Let us not mutiny against the hand of a loving Father.

We may faint under it (v. 5). If we fail to remember that the One who has sent the chastening *is with us in the midst of it* to carry us through, we may feel that the load is heavier than we can bear and become despondent. We may feel ourselves in a tunnel that has no end. The remedy is to lean harder on our burden-bearing God who knows our load-limit. The strength of the test is the measure of our ability to bear it (1 Cor. 10:13).

We should be in subjection (v. 9). "Besides this, we have had earthly fathers to discipline us and we respected them. Shall we not much more be subject to the Father of spirits and live?" (RSV).

This exhortation is easier to utter than to observe, yet there is no other way to deliverance and victory. Although we may not see the whole road ahead of us, we can still trust a wise Father. The lowest level of victory is to *submit* because we know resistance to the divine will is unavailing. To *acquiesce* in the loving wisdom of God's dealings with us is higher ground. But what brings most glory and joy to the heart of God, and most rest to the chastened soul, is to *embrace* the will of God with a song. To say "Even so, Father, for so it seemed good in Thy sight," though the voice is choked with sobs.

Madame Guyon, a brilliant and refined French lady, was flung into a gloomy, dirty dungeon in the Bastille, where she was imprisoned for several years. Denied everything to which she was accustomed, she so rose above her circumstances as to be able to describe her experience in these terms: "Even the very stones in

53

my prison floor shone like rubies in my eyes," so real was the presence of the Lord to her.

In her strange cage she composed songs of praise to God, one of which follows:

> A little bird am I,
>   Shut out from fields of air,
> Yet in my cage I sit and sing
>   To Him who placed me there,
> Well-pleased a prisoner to be
> Because, my Lord, it pleaseth Thee.
>
> Naught else have I to do,
>   I sing the whole day long,
> And He whom most I love to please
>   Doth listen to my song.
> He caught and bound my wandering wing,
> But still He loves to hear me sing.
>
> Oh, it is good to soar,
>   These bolts and bars above,
> To Him whose purpose I adore, /
>   Whose providence I love,
> And in His mighty will to find
> The joy and freedom of the mind.

THE CONSUMMATION OF LIFE'S DISCIPLINES

Discipline is not welcomed by carnality, and yet it is God's most valued instrument in perfecting human character. He is working to a plan—that we might be like His Son, of whom it is written: "Though he were a Son, yet learned he obedience by the things which he suffered" (Heb. 5:8).

Our great concern should be that every discipline God sends into our lives is taken advantage of and made to accomplish the divine purpose. Our Scripture reading indicates a fourfold consummation which should be the outcome of our disappointments and failures, our sorrow and suffering:

They prove our sonship (v. 8). So far from it being a proof of indifference or lack of love on the part of a parent who disciplines a child, the very reverse is the case. It is the fondest and most interested parent who devotes the greatest attention to the child's training and who, at the cost of personal pain, does not spare the rod, if that is better calculated to mold the character. It is an illuminating sidelight on suffering to know that "The Lord disciplines him whom he loves, and chastises every son whom he receives" (Heb. 12: 6, RSV).

> Only my Father knows
>   What chastening I need,
> Or what, in love, He'd teach to me,
>   Since I'm His "son indeed."
>
> Only my Father knows
>   The pain my soul must bear,
> Ere it be tuned to sing His praise,
>   And in His glory share.
>
> But since my Father's strength
>   Is mine — for all the years,
> I'll triumph in His chastening,
>   And praise Him through my tears.

They are for our profit (v. 10). God is not capricious in His dealings, nor does He cherish a grudge against any of His creatures. He is working with our eternal profit in view, although at times it seems as though it is for our loss. But this is only because we are blind and in the dark.

A bar of steel worth $2.00, when made into needles, increases its value to $150.00. If fashioned into knife blades, it is worth $13,000.00. If made into watch-springs, its value would be $100,000.00. What accounts for the enhanced value? The more it is hammered, beaten, manipulated, the more it endures of the fire, the greater is the value of the steel. "For our light affliction, which is but for a moment, worketh for us a far more exceeding and eternal weight of glory" (2 Cor. 4:17).

They produce holiness (v. 10). "Partakers of his holiness." What a consummation is this! If He was made perfect through suffering, how else can we be made partakers of His holiness? Trial does not make us holy automatically, whether we will it or not, but trial rightly received will sanctify us. Fire removes from the ore only that which detracts from its highest value, and the fires of testing remove only the sins and weights which, in sullying our holiness, inevitably mar our happiness.

They produce a harvest (v. 11). Too often the heavenly Husbandman has come to the tree of our lives looking for fruit, only to find "nothing but leaves." He desires not only fruit for His own delectation, but "fruit that may abound to [our] account" (Phil. 4:17).

Chastening is one of His most effective fertilizers. When He applies it, there is borne the precious fruit of *faith,* which trusts when it cannot see; of *peace,* which is tranquil in the midst of storm; of *longsuffering,* which bears and forbears even when sorely tried; and of *love,* which remains true even when seemingly forsaken.

If this consummation of our chastening and discipline is our earnest desire, we can reecho the prayer of Dr. Joseph Parker:

> Plough on, Lord, I want my life to be ploughed all over, and that in every corner there may be golden grain or glorious flowers. Pity me that I exclaimed when I first felt the plough-share; Thou knowest my frame. Thou rememberest that I am but dust; but now I recollect, I put things together, I see Thy meaning. *So drive on, Thou Ploughman of Eternity!*

MY GLORIOUS VICTOR!

My glorious Victor, Prince Divine,
Clasp these surrendered hands in Thine;
At length my will is all Thine own,
Glad vassal of a Saviour's throne.

My Master, lead me to Thy door;
Pierce this now willing ear once more;
My bonds are freedom; let me stay
With Thee to toil, endure, obey.

Yes, ear and hand, and thought and will,
Use all in Thy dear slav'ry still!
Self's weary liberties I cast
Beneath Thy feet; there keep them fast.

Tread them still down; and then I know,
These hands shall with Thy gifts o'erflow;
And pierced ears shall hear the tone
Which tells me Thou and I are one.

H. C. G. Moule

5 THE LORDSHIP OF CHRIST

> None of us lives to himself (but to the Lord), and
> none of us dies to himself (but to the Lord, for) If
> we live, we live to the Lord, and if we die, we die to
> the Lord. So then, whether we live or we die, we be-
> long to the Lord. For Christ died and lived again for
> this very purpose, that He might be Lord both of the
> dead and of the living.   Roman 14:7-9 (*Amplified*)

DEMOCRACY, THE RULE of the people by the people,
has not proved to be a panacea for all the world's ills.
In many countries where this mode of government has
been adopted, it has been abandoned in favor of a
military dictatorship, or some similar arrangement,
simply because it failed to meet the needs of the hour.
To some degree the people may have found it wise to
vest authority in the hands of an able man. The character of the man, of course, determines the character
of the regime.

In most spheres of life a similar pattern is followed.
Each army has a commander, each navy has an admiral, each ship a captain. Every kingdom has its king
and each home its head. Yet in the complex kingdom
of Man's soul, with all its baffling problems, it is fondly
dreamed that, with authority divided between Christ
and self, progress and victory may still be achieved.
The delusion is vain. He alone can confidently expect
victory in his life who has submitted unreservedly to
the Lordship, the mastery of Christ.

> Make me a captive, Lord,
>   And then I shall be free,
> Force me to render up my sword,
>   And I shall conqueror be.

It is surely a reasonable inference that if we can get
Jesus Christ into the same relative position in our lives

as He occupies in heaven, then the joy of heaven will be ours. What place does He occupy in heaven? "The Lamb . . . in the midst of the throne." If by our own deliberate choice Christ is placed on the throne of our lives, He will control and rule them beneficently.

THE BASIS OF CHRIST'S LORDSHIP

The fact of Christ's Lordship is *plainly declared* in Scripture. The central point in the Pentecostal sermon is this statement, "God hath made that same Jesus, whom ye have crucified, both LORD and Christ" (Acts 2:36). On the first occasion on which the name of Jesus was preached to the Gentiles, Peter asserted, "He is LORD of all" (Acts 10:36). His right to the Lordship and control of the lives of those who are united to Him by faith is not based upon our recognition of it or our endorsement of it, but upon the declaration that God has constituted Him Lord.

His position of Lordship is *richly deserved* in the light of His amazing self-abnegation and self-impoverishment for us. "Being in the form of God . . . [he] made himself of no reputation, and took upon him the form of a servant, and was made in the likeness of men; and being found in fashion as a man, he humbled himself, and became obedient unto death, even the death of the cross" (Phil. 2:6-8). And again, "Ye know the grace of our Lord Jesus Christ, that, though he was rich, yet for your sakes he became poor, that ye through his poverty might be rich" (2 Cor. 8:9).

Who that has followed his Lord down those steps of deepening humiliation enumerated by Paul would have the temerity to say that His claim to Lordship was undeserved? Who, looking through tears at His five bleeding wounds, would deny His worthiness of our utmost devotion? His self-oblation on Calvary entitles Him to wield the scepter over every redeemed heart.

The position as Lord of our lives is *earnestly desired* by Him. Indeed, this was the reason for His death and resurrection. It was not alone that *we* might experience salvation from hell in the future, but that *He* might be honored in the present as Lord of our lives.

This fact emerges clearly from Romans 14:9. "For to this end Christ both died, and rose, and revived, that he might be LORD both of the dead and living." The ultimate objective of Christ's death and resurrection was the winning of undisputed Lordship over those for whose sake He died and rose again. If this is denied Him, what can take its place? To refuse it is to rob Him of the fruit of His passion—to snatch from His lips the cup of joy that was set before Him.

Although Christ deserves and covets this position of absolute authority in the lives of His disciples, and although He would exercise His powers only for our blessing, His claim is all too often *disputed or denied*. In effect, if not in word, we say, "We will not have this man to reign over us." Not that we would for a moment blatantly use these words, but many who willingly accept life from Him refuse to let His word be their law. He may be hailed as *Savior* but ignored as *Sovereign*, and yet the one office is as clearly presented in Scripture as the other. Is it logically possible for us to accept Christ as Savior and reject Him as Lord? A. W. Tozer wrote: "It is altogether doubtful whether any man can be saved who comes to Christ for His help, but with no intention to obey Him."

The attitude of a non-Christian in refusing His Lordship is understandable, as when Mahatma Gandhi said, "I am unable to place Jesus Christ on a solitary throne," but it is tragic when those called by His name do this.

When at great personal sacrifice Garibaldi delivered Italy from the invading hordes, he was hailed as the savior of the nation. No flattery could be too fulsome, no praise too extreme for the national hero.

One party maintained that the logical recognition of such service was to place him on the throne and entrust him with the scepter of empire. Others, however, although eagerly embracing the benefits accruing from his victory, disputed his right to sovereignty. For some days he was actually put in prison by the very people he had saved from annihilation. Instead of occupying the throne, he was banished to the Island of Capri, which was presented to him later in recognition of his services, when the country came to its senses. But what a recompense for such self-sacrificing heroism!

Is our Lord not sometimes treated in the same manner? His Saviorhood is welcomed, but He Himself is banished to some backroom of the heart, while self is allowed to usurp His throne. Is our allegiance divided? Do we dispute His Lordship?

THE IMPLICATIONS OF HIS LORDSHIP

"Sanctify in your hearts Christ as LORD" (1 Pet. 3: 15, RV).

The first implication of these words is that on our part there must be *entire submission*. If He is indeed Lord of our lives, our attitude will be one of glad submission and obedience. Like Christ, we will say, "I delight to do Thy will, O my God."

> My will is not my own
> Till Thou hast made it Thine,
> If it would reach the monarch's throne,
> It must its crown resign.

After a notable British victory over the French in naval battle, the defeated French admiral smilingly approached Lord Nelson with hand outstretched and sword swinging at his side. Nelson impassively greeted the French admiral with, "Your sword first, sir." Before friendly relations could be established, all arms of rebellion must be surrendered. As Lord, Christ demands and is entitled to undivided allegiance and submission.

His Lordship implies *absolute ownership* of the believer and all that he has. "He is Lord of *all*," affirmed Peter. Everything we have is His by right of creation. It has become doubly His because purchased by His

62

blood. We are not our own; we have been bought with the price of His sacrifice.

All that I have and am,
Thy gifts so free —

Enumerate them in His presence—possessions, business, home, treasures, money, investments, friends, husband, wife, children, lover, intellect, abilities, recreations—all are from Him and are to be enjoyed and used for His glory. If His absolute ownership is not acknowledged, His reign is merely nominal.

Ananias and Sapphira endeavored to emulate those believers to whom Christ's ownership of all was so real that they sold their possessions and laid the proceeds at the feet of His apostles. But they made the tragic blunder of professing to give all to God, while secretly keeping back part for their own enjoyment. They were not obliged to give all, but they desired to have a reputation for generosity which was undeserved. Their hypocrisy brought condign judgment on them. We, too, may be guilty of professing to recognize Christ's absolute ownership while denying it in practice.

Sir John Ramsden, as a young man, established his cotton mill in the small English town of Huddersfield. As his business prospered, he bought up increasing areas to enlarge his mill and accommodate his workmen. Eventually he was able to purchase the whole of the town with the exception of one house, right in its center, which was owned by an old Quaker.

Through the years Sir John's agents had approached the Quaker again and again with tempting offers, but he could not be persuaded to sell his home. At last Sir John determined to pay a personal visit and to make an offer the Quaker could not refuse.

"I suppose you know who I am," said Sir John.

"Oh yes, I know who thee art," replied the Quaker.

"And I suppose you can guess why I am here?"

"Oh yes, I can guess why thee art here."

"Well, I will make you a very generous offer for

your house. If you will sell it to me, I will cover the land with golden sovereigns."

For a few moments the Quaker was silent, and then with a quizzical smile he said, "If thee wilt put them edgewise, we might talk business."

Angry and crestfallen, Sir John turned on his heel and left the house. When he had reached the gate, the old Quaker called after him,

"Remember, Sir John, that Huddersfield belongs to thee *and to me.*"

In every life where Christ's claims to Lordship are recognized in general but are denied in some area, small or large, a similar position arises. The devil can say, "Remember, Christ, that that man whom You purchased with Your blood on Calvary belongs to You *and to me,*" for Satan retains vested interests in every area of life we exclude from Christ's sway.

The believer who recognizes Christ's Lordship, will yield Him *unquestioning obedience.* His own challenging words make this crystal clear: "Why call ye me, Lord, Lord, and do not the things which I say?" (Luke 6:46).

Disobedience vitiates all professed recognition of His Lordship. What we perform drowns the voice of what we profess. A soldier in the army is allowed one sixth of a second from the issuing of the command in which to prove his obedience to his senior officer. Is our obedience to our Lord equally prompt and unquestioning? We should cultivate the habit of saying an unhesitating, "Yes, Lord," in all things and at all times, however costly the obedience may be.

Speaking of a crisis in his life when he fully yielded to Christ's control, E. J. Pace the Christian cartoonist said, "I never dreamed of the enrichment that has been mine, when thirty-five years ago I made over all to Christ. He has taken the frown out of my obedience."

Christ's claim to Lordship will involve *divine disturbance,* for He will exercise it when we concede it to Him. His scepter will not be a mere symbol. While

His reign will involve disturbance in some areas of life, it will be "for our good always." His antagonism is only to that which is sinful, and his interventions will be harbingers of blessing. Were it not for Calvary, we might fear the sovereignty of Christ.

The results will vary in different lives. It may be in the realm of literature of a certain type, or the viewing of certain programs which are not conducive to spiritual progress. It may be in the expenditure of money in unnecessary or self-indulgent ways. It may be in a new and careful stewardship of time, or in the breaking of an unhelpful relationship. The sovereign Lord will brook no rival. He will take second place to nothing and no one, for "He is *Lord of all.*"

THE RECOGNITION OF HIS LORDSHIP

Christ employs no press-gang to procure soldiers for His army. He looks for volunteers. In time of war, when recruits are called for, the man who does not enlist is not deprived of his rights of citizenship. He merely does not respond to his country's call to service. So also in these days of bitter spiritual conflict, the Christian who does not respond to Christ's claim to Lordship of his life is not deprived of his heavenly citizenship. He simply refuses service under the banner of his King, and thereby forfeits joy in the present and undreamed of reward in the future.

A clear and definite activity of the will is involved in recognizing His Lordship, since He is to be Lord of all. By her "I will," the bride at the marriage altar, ideally, forever enthrones her groom in her affections. In subsequent years she lives out in detail all that was implied in that momentary act of will. A similar enthronement of Christ can result from a similar act of will, for the same decision as enthrones Christ automatically dethrones Self.

It is here that, for many, a practical problem arises. How can we not only enthrone Christ as Lord, but maintain our recognition of His Lordship? Our wills are so weak, and we have known failure at this point so often in the past.

The answer is found in these words, "No man can say"—keep on saying, is the significance of the tense—"that Jesus Christ is Lord but by the Holy Spirit" (1 Cor. 12:3). It is obvious that this verse does not mean that it is impossible for a man merely to say these words apart from the Holy Spirit, but that he cannot concede to Christ His position of Lordship and consistently maintain that attitude, apart from the enabling of the Holy Spirit. If this is our aspiration, it can be achieved by His inspiration.

The method of securing the Spirit's cooperation is clearly stated:

"If ye then, being evil know how to give good gifts to your children, how much more shall your heavenly Father give the Holy Spirit"—in His attributes and operations—"to them that *ask* him" (Luke 11:13).

"And this is the confidence that we have in him, that, if we *ask* any thing according to his will, he heareth us, and . . . we know that we have the petitions that we desired of him" (1 John 5:14, 15).

"*Ask* and ye shall receive that your joy may be full" (John 16:24).

The Holy Spirit alone can present and enforce Christ's claim to Lordship of our hearts, but He who has created the desire will enable the coronation. He will detach our affections from the world and its allurements and attach them to Christ, as we trust Him to do it. He will impart the daily grace to take up the cross and follow Him. The mighty Holy Spirit can be relied on to enable us to keep on saying that Jesus Christ is our Lord.

His activities do not cease on the accomplishment of that first act of coronation. He will constantly discover to us new territories in our lives that are to be brought under Christ's imperial scepter, for there is room for endless progress in the Christian life. He will apply the principle of progressive surrender to yet larger areas of our lives as we yield to His working.

It remains within our power to withhold our lives from Christ's sovereign control, to refuse to "bring forth the royal diadem, and crown Him Lord of all," but at a tragic cost. The full potentiality of our lives will never be realized.

The organist in a village church in Germany was playing some music of Mendelssohn, and was not playing it very well. A stranger, hearing the music, crept into the church and sat in the dimness of the back pew, where he heard the imperfections of the organist's performance. When he ceased playing and prepared to depart, the stranger said, "Sir, would you allow me to play the organ for a little while?"

"Certainly not," was the surly answer. "I never allow anyone to touch the organ but myself."

"I should be so grateful if you would give me the privilege," persisted the stranger.

Again he met with gruff refusal. The third time his appeal was allowed, but most ungraciously.

The stranger sat down, adjusted the stops, and began to play the same piece, but with what a difference. It seemed as if the whole church was filled with heavenly music.

The organist looked askance and asked, "Who are you?"

Modestly the stranger replied, "I am Mendelssohn."

"What," cried the organist in deep mortification, "did I refuse *you* permission to play on my organ?"

That is what we do with Christ when we refuse Him the opportunity to take the instrument of our redeemed personalities, and bring out the harmonies of heaven.

I SURRENDER ALL

Laid on Thine altar, O my Lord divine,
  Accept the gift today, for Jesus' sake.
I have no jewels to adorn Thy shrine,
  Nor any world-famed sacrifice to make;
But here I bring within my trembling hand,
  This will of mine, a thing that seemeth small—
And Thou alone, O Lord, canst understand
  How when I yield Thee this, I yield mine all.

Hidden therein Thy searching gaze can see
  Struggles of passion, visions of delight,
All that I have, or am, or fain would be;
  Deep loves, fond hopes, and longings infinite;
It hath been wet with tears and dimmed with sighs,
  Clenched in my grasp till beauty hath it none!
Now from Thy footstool, where it vanquished lies,
  The prayer ascendeth—may Thy will be done!

Take it, O Father, ere my courage fail,
  And merge it so in Thine own will that e'en
If in some desperate hour my cries prevail,
  And Thou give back my gift it may have been
So changed, so purified, so fair have grown,
  So one with Thee, so filled with peace divine,
I may not know or feel it as my own,
  But, gaining back my will, may find it Thine.

6 THE YIELDED LIFE

> I plead with you therefore, brethren, by the compassions of God, to present all your faculties to Him as a living and holy sacrifice acceptable to Him. This with you will be an act of reasonable worship.
>
> Romans 12:1 (Weymouth)

> In full and glad surrender
> I give myself to Thee,
> Thine utterly and only,
> And evermore to be.

THIS IS THE ONLY language possible to the Christian who realizes something of the costliness to God of the sacrifice by which he has been redeemed.

Each has to decide what kind of Christian life he will live. On the one hand, it can be a life of self-pleasing and self-indulgence; a life in which Christ has a place, or even prominence, but not pre-eminence. On the other hand, it can be a life absolutely yielded to Christ, when His will is his delight; where self-pleasing is renounced and self-will crucified.

At first blush the former life seems the more attractive, and holds out greater promise of enjoyment. But when embarked upon, its promise fails to materialize. Its proffered pleasures turn to ashes in the mouth. Life seems empty and meaningless. The latter life, viewed superficially, appears difficult and exacting—and it is — but once entered upon, it proves a life of true joy and liberty. It is for such a life of full consecration that the Holy Spirit is pleading in this significant verse.

THE LANGUAGE OF CONSECRATION—*"I plead with you"*

The yielded life is entered upon in response to a divine call, as the history of the saints of all ages will confirm. In the case of some, the call comes in the crisis of conversion, but with the majority, at some later period in life. There is tender and winsome entreaty in Paul's appeal—"I plead with you." This was a favorite note with the apostle, as with his Master. He was not arguing or lecturing, he entreated on Christ's behalf. It reads as though the Lord is kneeling at the feet of His willful, self-pleasing child, pleading with him to yield his life to the control of One whose wisdom is unlimited and whose love passes knowledge.

THE SUBJECTS OF CONSECRATION — *"Brethren"*

The appeal of this verse is addressed to those who, through faith in Christ, have become children of God, and whom Christ is not ashamed to call "brethren." The divine order is first the yielding of the heart, and then of the body. When we respond to the first appeal, "My son, give me thy heart," He then pleads with us to yield our bodies, which can be the instruments either of sin or of righteousness. Those who are not Christ's, are "dead in sin," and therefore are not the subjects of consecration.

THE MOTIVE OF CONSECRATION—*"By the compassions of God"*

Such a drastic and revolutionary change in the life as the shifting of its center from self to Christ, must necessarily have powerful motivation. When we discover how deeply entrenched the self-life is in our hearts and wills, we may well despair of finding such a motive in ourselves. The text assures us that the adequate motive is found, not in ourselves, but in "the compassions of God."

To discover what these "mercies" or "compassions" are, it will be necessary to skip back over the parenthetical chapters nine to eleven of the Romans Letter, and search in its doctrinal section, chapters one to eight. What a galaxy of undeserved "compassions" confronts us!

70

An assurance of pardon for the past

"Blessed are those whose iniquities are forgiven and whose sins are covered" (Rom. 4:7).

An assertion of peace in the present

"Therefore being justified by faith we have peace with God through our Lord Jesus Christ" (Rom. 5:1). *glorified*

An assurance of power for the future

"Yield yourselves unto God, as those that are alive from the dead, and your members as instruments of righteousness unto God. For sin shall not have dominion over you" (Rom. 6:14, 15).

These are samples of the manifold mercies of which the apostle is speaking, and are they not of such a magnitude as to provide a powerful motive to yield our lives to the One who has imparted them?

> But drops of grief can ne'er repay
> The debt of love I owe;
> Dear Lord, I give myself away,
> 'Tis all that I can do.

THE METHOD OF CONSECRATION—*"To present"*

There are no conscripts in Christ's army. Each soldier is a volunteer who has responded to a call. Service motivated solely by a sense of duty is not acceptable to Him. The act of presentation for which Paul is pleading, is an act of the unfettered human will which has so often chosen contrary to its own highest interests.

The verb "present" is in the aorist tense, with its significance of a crisis, an act done now, once and for all. It need not be *repeated* at a monthly consecration meeting or at an annual convention. It may, and should, however, be *reaffirmed* if we realize that this is rendered necessary through coldness of heart. If a married couple have a quarrel, it is not necessary for them to be married again. If they are wise, they will make mutual confession, and reaffirm the vows they took at the marriage altar. Like the marriage covenant, this act of presentation is too sacred to be broken.

71

The presentation of our bodies is the renunciation of all right of control over them. We recognize that they are not our own, for they have been purchased at the stupendous cost of the life-blood of Christ our Lord, in whose service they are to be employed.

THE AREA OF CONSECRATION—*"Your bodies—all your faculties"*

Why our bodies? Why not our hearts, or our minds, or our spirits? These bodies of clay are surely not a worthy present for the King of Kings. Paul tells us why it is we should yield our bodies to God.

"What, know ye not that your bodies are the temple of the Holy Spirit which is in you, which ye have of God, and ye are not your own? For ye are bought with a price: Therefore glorify God in your body, and in your spirit, which are God's" (1 Cor. 6:19, 20).

Our bodies have the high privilege of housing the Holy Spirit and becoming the vehicle of His Self-expression. Each member has its part to play. "Yield yourselves unto God, as those that are alive from the dead, *and your members* as instruments of righteousness unto God" (Rom. 6:13). God desires that our whole being be placed entirely at His disposal. Not our time, our talents, our money merely, but *ourselves.*

> All for Jesus, all for Jesus,
>   All my being's ransomed powers;
> All my thoughts and words and doings,
>   All my days and all my hours.
>
> Let my hands perform His bidding;
>   Let my feet run in His ways;
> Let mine eyes see Jesus only;
>   Let my lips speak forth His praise.

A preacher made a stirring appeal for a sacrificial love offering for work among the spiritually deprived people in foreign lands. Many in the congregation were deeply moved and gave liberally. In the audience was a small Negro boy whose heart had also been stirred, but he had no money to give. In what way could he respond?

His distress grew more acute as the collection plate drew nearer; then suddenly he was at peace. To the amazement of the elder who handed him the plate, the boy placed it on the floor and stood in it. This simple act of presenting his body, of self-surrender, melted the whole congregation to deep emotion. Like the Macedonians, he first gave himself to the Lord. May we cease to withhold our dearly-bought bodies from the One who purchased them with crimson drops of blood, and instead say,

> O Son of God who lov'st me,
>   I will be Thine alone,
> And all I have and all I am
>   Shall henceforth be Thine own.
>
> Reign over me Lord Jesus!
>   O make my heart Thy throne!
> It shall be Thine dear Saviour,
>   It shall be Thine alone.

THE QUALITY OF CONSECRATION—*"A living sacrifice"*

The dead blood-sacrifices of the Old Covenant are contrasted with the "living sacrifice" of the New. It is not simply making sacrifices for Christ that is indicated, although that too may be involved. It is something deeper and more fundamental. It would be far easier to die once for Christ than to do what is asked here—to become a life-long sacrifice offered up daily on the cross for His sake.

Paul affirmed, "I die daily." When Jesus was calling men to be His disciples, He never concealed the offense of the cross. He never promised them a primrose-strewn path. Instead, He threw out a challenge: "If any man will come after me, let him deny himself, and take up his cross daily and follow me" (Luke 9:23). Later in the same chapter He gently rebuffed those who volunteered to follow Him without first counting the cost. The yielded life is one of constant self-sacrifice, but it is also a life of sublimest joy.

Our Lord never asks of us something which He has not done Himself. His whole life was one long sacrificing of Himself, which found its culmination in the supreme sacrifice of the cross. He says, "Follow me," implying that He Himself has trodden the path before us.

The step of presentation lengthens out into a walk of constant surrender. It is to be a *living* sacrifice, and life involves progress. Our responsibility is to present to God all that we know He asks of us at the present moment. If we obey the light He gives up to our present knowledge, the Holy Spirit will reveal fresh areas which we can yield to Him.

Dr. J. Wilbur Chapman once said to General Booth, founder of the Salvation Army, "Tell me, what has been the secret of your great success?"

General Booth answered simply, "So far as I know God has had all there was of me. There have been men with greater brains, greater opportunities than I, but from the day I had a vision of what God could do with poor old London, I made up my mind that God would have all there was of William Booth." From this statement Dr. Chapman learned that the greatness of a man's power is the measure of his surrender. General Booth had presented his life a *living sacrifice,* and the world saw the result.

THE CHARACTER OF CONSECRATION—*"Holy"*

The believer who is yielded to God becomes henceforth utterly devoted to Him. He voluntarily and gladly turns from the world and its allurements, and is separated to Christ. He has made a final break with sin, as from a master to whom willing service has been rendered, and his life now brings forth "fruit unto holi-

74

ness." Henceforth his life-motto is, "To me to live is *Christ.*"

> Jesus calls to separation,
> And Himself has led the way;
> His own life the explanation,
> His own life the illustration,
> Who is willing to obey?

THE OBJECT OF CONSECRATION — *"Acceptable unto God"*

The yielding of the believer's life to God should not be made merely in hope of material gain or personal enjoyment. Nor should it be prompted by fear of personal loss or suffering, but from a sincere desire to be well-pleasing to God. This is the meaning of the word "acceptable." The yielding of our "being's ransomed powers" brings pleasure to God! This is surely adequate compensation for any cost involved. With what alacrity would the angels seize the opportunity which is ours, were it offered to them. And if we bring pleasure to God, then at the same time we minister to our own happiness, for God's joy and ours are inextricably intertwined.

THE SANITY OF CONSECRATION—*"An Act of reasonable worship"*

When He pleads for an absolute surrender of our bodies to Him, Christ is not making an unreasonable demand. In his translation of this verse A. S. Way underlines this phrase: "The necessity of this rite of consecration follows from all the argument." It is the logical issue of our acceptance of all the blessings that flow from our union with Christ. It is reasonable, for God has been pleased to use human instrumentality in achieving His purposes of blessing for the world of men. It is reasonable in view of what we owe to our God as those who have been bought by blood.

75

This transaction once completed, our lives can never be the same again. We will still be fallible mortals and subject to many human limitations, but with this difference. The indwelling Holy Spirit can now exert unhindered control of our bodies and their members. Through us He can work in power. Our human weakness need be no hindrance. "All God's giants have been weak men who did great things for God, because they reckoned on God being with them," said Hudson Taylor.

When opening a campaign in New York, D. L. Moody said, "When God wants to move a mountain, He does not take a bar of iron, but a little worm (Isa. 41:14, 15). The fact is, we have got too much strength. We are not weak enough. It is not our strength that we need. One drop of God's strength is worth more than all human power."

One early morning in Dublin, a company of men gathered for a time of prayer and renewed consecration. Among them was Grattan Guinness, the noted missionary, Henry Varley, an evangelist, and D. L. Moody. Quietly and in deep humility, at a hushed interval, Varley said, "The world has yet to see what God can do with and for and through and in a man who is fully consecrated to Him."

This unrehearsed remark greatly moved Moody. Two days later, as he was listening to a sermon by Charles Haddon Spurgeon, Varley's statement was revolving in his mind. Here are his own words: "A man; Varley meant *any* man. Varley didn't say he had to be educated, or brilliant or anything else! Just a man! Well, by the Holy Spirit in him, he'd be *one* of those men.

"And then, suddenly, in that high gallery, he saw something he had never realized before—it was not Mr. Spurgeon, after all, who was doing the work, but God. And if God could use Mr. Spurgeon, why should He not use the rest of us, and why should we not all just lay ourselves at the Master's feet, and say to Him, 'Send me! Use me!' "

God will not make of us a Moody or a Spurgeon or a Billy Graham, but if we respond to the fervent appeal of this text, He will make us "vessels meet for the Master's use."

IN MY HEART AT LAST

Thou who givest of Thy gladness
  Till the cup runs o'er—
Cup whereof the pilgrim weary
  Drinks to thirst no more—
Not a-nigh me, but within me
  Is Thy joy divine;
Thou, O Lord, hast made Thy dwelling
  In this heart of mine.

Need I that a law should bind me
  Captive unto Thee?
Captive is my heart, rejoicing
  Never to be free.
Ever with me, glorious, awful,
  Tender, passing sweet,
One upon whose heart I rest me,
  Worship at His feet.

With me, wheresoe'er I wander,
  That great Presence goes,
That unutterable gladness,
  Undisturbed repose.
Everywhere the blessed stillness
  Of His Holy Place—
Stillness of the love that worships
  Dumb before His face.

To Thy house, O God my Father,
  Thy lost child is come;
Led by wandering lights no longer,
  I have found my home.
Over moor and fen I tracked them
  Through the midnight blast,
But to find the Light eternal
  In my heart at last.

Gerhard Tersteegen

7 THE INDWELLING OF CHRIST

> Know ye not that Jesus Christ is in you?
> 2 Corinthians 13:5
>
> Christ liveth in me.   Galatians 2:20

ONE UNIQUE CHARACTERISTIC of Christianity as compared with other religions, is that it is the only religion in which the Founder claims to *live in* the person who believes in Him. He claims to influence His followers, not from without but from within. This teaching and this experience are peculiar to Christianity, and constitute its supreme glory.

The indwelling of Christ in the believer is one of the very important doctrines of the New Testament. It may sound mystical, but the presence of the living Christ in the believing heart is blessedly real. Just as the sap indwells the branch, producing luscious fruit, just as the blood indwells the body, manifesting itself in abundant life, so Christ dwells in the depth of the believer's spirit, to reproduce His own attractive character.

Writing of his own experience, Dr. G. Campbell Morgan said: "Christ in me is the most certain thing in all my personal experience. He is present in my inner life. I do not have to make a pilgrimage to find Him. He was not always there. He came by the act of the Holy Spirit, when I complied with God's conditions of salvation. The historical is proved by the experimental." This serious testimony of a serious scholar cannot lightly be dismissed.

> I need not journey far
> This distant Friend to see;
> Companionship is always mine,
> He makes His home with me.

79

I envy not the twelve;
Nearer to me is He,
The life that once He lived on earth
He lives again in me.

The New Testament speaks of two mysteries of surpassing greatness. On Paul's lips, "mystery" carried a meaning almost the opposite of what we attach to it today. The word, borrowed from contemporary religions, as used by them signified, "a truth or rite reserved for only the select circle of the initiated." But when used by Paul, the word had a different meaning—a sacred secret, long hidden, and impenetrable to man, who could learn it only by divine revelation.

The heathen "mysteries" could be known to only the favored few. But the mysteries of which Paul speaks are open to "every man in Christ" (Col. 1:28) —not to a limited spiritual aristocracy. There is no favored class in Christianity.

The first of the two mysteries is *the incarnation of God in the human nature of Christ.* "Great is the mystery of godliness . . . . God was manifest in the flesh . . ." (1 Tim. 3:16). Mystery of mysteries, the Infinite becomes an infant! "Made in the likeness of men."

The second mystery is even greater, *the incarnation of Christ in the life of the consecrated believer.* "To whom God would make known what is the riches of the glory of this mystery, which is *Christ in you,* the hope of glory" (Col. 1:27). The language Paul uses makes it seem as though he is overcome with awe at the wonder of this marvelous secret.

This first mystery, Christ *for* us, is the basis of our salvation. The second, Christ *in* us, is the basis of our sanctification.

Before we turn to the more practical aspects of our theme, let us examine its Scriptural foundations. The indwelling of Christ is

It was foreshadowed in the Old Testament. The word of the Lord to Israel was, "And I will set my tabernacle among you, and I will walk among you, and will be your God" (Lev. 26:11, 12). In making use of this passage, Paul wrote, "As God hath said, *I will dwell in them,* and I will be their God" (2 Cor. 6:16).

It was foretold by Christ Himself in cryptic words: "He that eateth my flesh and drinketh my blood, *dwelleth in me and I in him"* (John 6:56). But His disciples could not grasp His meaning. And why did they not understand? Because this truth can be apprehended only through the illumination of the Holy Spirit, and at this time, "the Holy Spirit was not yet given, because Jesus was not yet glorified" (John 7:39). We shall be just as impotent as they to grasp the glorious fact that Christ actually, literally indwells us, if He is not glorified in our lives, and the Spirit does not make Him real to us.

On that memorable night in the upper room, Jesus revealed the mystery in still clearer terms.

"At that day" — when the Spirit is given — "ye shall know that I am in my Father, and ye in me, *and I in you"* (John 14:20).

"He that abideth in me *and I in him"* (John 15:5).

"That the love wherewith thou hast loved me may be in them, *and I in them"* (John 17:26).

These statements make it crystal clear that the Lover of our souls will not rest content with mere exterior contact with the objects of His love. He will actually dwell in the heart that reciprocates His affection.

It is further developed in the epistles of Paul and John:

"If Christ be in you, the body is dead because of sin" (Rom. 8:10).

81

"Know ye not that *Jesus Christ is in you* . . ." (2 Cor. 13:5).

"Christ liveth in me . . ." (Gal. 2:20).

"That *Christ may dwell in your heart* by faith" (Eph. 3:17).

"Christ in you, the hope of glory" (Col. 1:27).

"Greater is *he that is in you,* than he that is in the world" (1 John 4:4).

The question we must ask and answer is whether this imposing array of Scripture has any corresponding reality in our experience. Do we have a distant Christ who pays us occasional visits, or is His personal, continuous indwelling a matter of conscious reality? It is impossible to read the Acts of the Apostles without being impressed by the fact that to the early Christians Jesus was vividly real and near.

It is regrettable that Dr. Bonar's beautiful but poignant poem describes the experience of so many.

> Sometimes I catch sweet glimpses of His face,
>   But that is all.
> Sometimes He speaks a passing word of peace,
>   But that is all.
> Sometimes I think I hear His loving voice,
>   Upon me call.
>
> And is this *all* He meant when thus He spake,
>   Come unto Me?
> Is there no deeper, more enduring rest
>   In Him for thee?
> Is there no steadier light for thee in Him?
>   O come and see!

It has been experienced by saints in all ages. What transformed the timid, jealous, self-seeking disciples into courageous, self-effacing ambassadors of Christ? *Pentecost,* when the risen Christ was made gloriously real to them. Cowardice, envy and self-seeking were expelled from hearts in which Christ had been invited to make His home.

When did Paul's career in all its flaming grandeur

really begin? Was it when he was blinded by the brilliance of the revelation of Christ on the Damascus road? That certainly was a tremendous crisis. But his marvelous career began not with a merely *external* revelation of Christ. He speaks of experiencing an *internal* revelation—"When it pleased God *to reveal his Son in me,*" or "within my soul" (Gal. 1:16). He had already seen Christ, exalted at the right hand of God, but now He was revealed to him as dwelling in his unworthy heart. Now he was able to say, "I live, yet not I, but *Christ liveth in me*" (Gal. 2:20). He was able to conquer sin, endure hardness and achieve the incredible, not through his mere human talents, but through Christ in him.

It should be noted that in Paul's experience, "Christ liveth in me" was preceded by, "I have been crucified with Christ." Our lives can be a fresh incarnation of Christ only in so far as we yield the old self-life to the death of the cross, as we consent to live a crucified, self-denying life. Then the Holy Spirit is able to reveal the Lord within, no longer an external Christ but an indwelling Savior.

> O to be saved from myself, dear Lord,
> O to be lost in Thee,
> O that it may be no more I
> But Christ that lives in me.

The indwelling of Christ is a fact to know, an experience to realize and a testimony to share:

A FACT TO KNOW

Not a promise to claim, but a fact to be believed and counted on as true. Not a dream of Pantheism or of the divine immanence, not a figure of speech or a figment of imagination, but a solid dependable fact.

"Know ye not that Jesus Christ *is in you*" (2 Cor. 13:5).

"He that *is in you*" (1 John 4:4).

Some may protest that this is beyond their experience, and that they have no consciousness of Christ within. We admit there is an element of the mystical about this truth, but there are mysterious facts that we accept without question.

Do we understand how the soul inhabits the body? Are we conscious of the blood flowing through our veins? If we are, we should see the physician! Yet we have no problem in accepting these facts and living with the mystery.

There is a difference between a fact and the consciousness of that fact. Indeed, in this case the acceptance of the fact precedes the enjoyment of the experience, for Christ dwells in our hearts by faith, and faith must always have a fact to rest upon.

"It is my confident belief," wrote F. B. Meyer, "that there is not a single man or woman who believes in Christ who has not Christ in the heart; but remember, that as the heavy veil hid the holy of holies from the holy place, so Jesus Christ may be in your heart, but because you have never recognized that He is there, because you have made no use of His presence there, because you have been unbelieving . . . . His presence has been hidden from your eyes; it has been veiled. I pray God that the two hands that rent the veil of the temple in twain from the top to the bottom, may rend the veil in your inner life, that Christ who is there, may be revealed to you."

Though living in this post-Pentecostal age, some Christians are in reality living in a pre-Pentecostal spiritual experience. Like the disciples, they have the experience of Christ *with* them, but they have no abiding experience of Christ *in* them, because they either do not know or do not believe the fact of Christ's indwelling. The first step is to accept as true the clearly revealed fact, and then it will be possible to go on to the experience.

Alexander Maclaren, prince of Bible expositors, had no doubt as to this fact. He said, "Let me say in the plainest, simplest, strongest way I can, that *the dwelling of Christ in the believing heart is to be regarded as a plain literal fact.* It is not to be weakened down into any participation in His likeness, following His example or the like.

"A dead Plato may so influence his followers, but that is not how a living Christ influences His disciples. . . . This indwelling may be a permanent and unbroken one . . . .

"Oh! what a contrast to that idea of a perpetual, unbroken habitation of Jesus in our spirit and to our consciousness, is presented by our ordinary life! God means and wishes that Christ may continuously dwell in our hearts. Does He to your own consciousness dwell in yours?"

The indwelling Christ is also

An Experience to Realize

Paul's prayer for the Ephesians, "that Christ may dwell in your heart by faith," at first blush seems to contradict what has just been said. It has been asserted that the indwelling of Christ is a fact whether we are conscious of it or not. And yet in this verse Paul is praying that they might have this experience. If Christ is already in their hearts, why pray for it to take place?

The explanation is not far to seek. In the Corinthian passage, Paul was emphasizing a fact. In Ephesians, he is exhorting them to go on to an experience. The key to the problem lies in the word "dwell," which carries the idea of settling down, of settled residence. Kenneth Wuest translates the verse, "That the Christ might settle down and be completely at home in your heart, through your faith." Granted that the Lord is in me, *but is He at home in me?* One can be in a house without being "at home" in it!

To be at home ideally implies the absence of tension and strain, mutual confidence, easy relationships, a loving welcome at all times. Is Christ able to settle down in our hearts as His permanent home?

Again, the word "dwell" in this verse is in the aorist tense, indicating a final, decisive act. It indicates an experience that could be crucial. It is not a merely intellectual conception, for Paul does not say "that Christ may dwell in your *mind,*" but "in your *heart.*" In the New Testament, "heart" would include the subconscious as well as the conscious. When Christ is at home in the heart, He is able to illumine the intellect, purify the imagination, control the emotions and reinforce the will, from within.

Does it seem impossible that the sense of His indwelling presence could be a constant reality in the midst of the pressing duties of daily life? It is far from impossible, as familiar analogies will show.

A man takes his account books home at night to catch up on some pressing work. His wife is at his side reading. Although his mind is fully engrossed with the columns of figures he is adding—and a man cannot think of his wife while adding figures—is he not all the time enjoying her presence, though not giving her a conscious thought?

While a mother is concentrating on her household work and her mind is fully occupied, is she not all the time conscious of the presence of the baby in its basinette? It does not take a special effort of her mind to induce this consciousness. Why? Because man is heart as well as mind — and Christ dwells not in the mind only, but in the heart, in response to our faith.

To the merchant engaged in solving the absorbing problems of his business, the consciousness of Christ's presence in the depths of his spirit can be just as real as when his mind is free to dwell on the sublime fact. The mind may be fully occupied and yet the heart joyously conscious of the presence of the indwelling Lord.

> More present to faith's vision keen,
> Than any earthly object seen,
> More dear, more intimately nigh
> Than e'en the closest earthly tie.

If it be asked, "How does the experience come?" the question is answered in the text: "That Christ may

dwell in your heart *in response to your faith.*" Enjoying the experience involves the activity of faith.
Faith takes its stand on the revealed fact, believes it
to be true, and appropriates the indwelling Christ for
every need. It is in the *believing* heart where He is welcomed and wanted, that Christ takes up His abode,
and the Holy Spirit makes His presence vividly real.
"By this we have proof that He really lives in us, by
the Holy Spirit who is given to us" (1 John 3:24,
Amplified). And is not this exactly what Jesus said?
"At that day" — when the Spirit is given — *"ye shall
know* that I am in you" (John 14:20). In Henry
Martyn's diary of his experiences in India, he wrote,
"My principal enjoyment is the enjoyment of Christ's
presence."

The indwelling Christ provides

A TESTIMONY TO SHARE

Paul's union with Christ was no mystical thing, but
a fact of real and momentary experience. So entirely
one with Christ did Paul become in his inner experience that he claimed, "To me to live is *Christ.*" Not
to be Christ-like, or to have Christ's help, but *Christ.*
His life and Christ's had fused in an indissoluble union
of thought and feeling. Christ had constituted Himself
Paul's very life.

The indwelling Christ will, of course, make His
presence felt. If as he claimed, the old Paul no longer
lived but Christ lived in his renewed personality, we
would expect him to grow increasingly like his indwelling Guest.

Was his Lord consumed with a love for the lost?
Then it is not surprising to hear Paul's testimony coming from a burdened heart, "I could wish that myself
were accursed from Christ for my brethren, my kins-
men according to the flesh" (Rom. 9:3). Did Christ
live a life of unappreciated self-sacrifice? Then His
bondslave manifests the same disposition. "I will very
gladly spend and be spent for you, though the more

abundantly I love you, the less I be loved" (2 Cor. 12:15).

Paul joyously shared his testimony to this experience with the Galatian believers: "It is no longer I that live, but Christ liveth in me." There is no suggestion here of the obliteration of personality. Our human personality is not displaced by the indwelling of Christ, as the fledglings of a thrush might be displaced by a cuckoo. Rather is it the inter-penetration of the human nature by the Divine. The human personality voluntarily and purposefully becomes the home of Christ. Self-consciousness is constantly blended with Christ-consciousness. It is enriched and empowered by the presence of Christ. "If Christ lives in us He can *overcome* for us, He can *overflow* from us, and life becomes the *outliving* of His inliving."

It is the office of the Holy Spirit to reproduce in our lives the graces and qualities that reside in their fullness in Christ who lives within. Do we lack love, or patience, or peace, or purity, or power, or courage, or joy? We may draw it from the One within. There is no need to envy the experience of the disciples whose hearts burned within them on their memorable walk to Emmaus. They entertained Him for only one night. We may entertain Him all day long, enjoying His unclouded presence.

Dr. A. B. Simpson, great preacher and missionary, termed this truth, "God's greatest secret of holy living," and bore testimony to it in verse and in prose.

"It is a great secret," he wrote, "which has been to me so wonderful. A good many years ago I came to Him, burdened with fear and guilt; I took that simple secret, and it took away all my fear and sin. Years passed on, and I found sin overcame me, and my temptations were too strong for me. I came to Him a second time, and He whispered to me 'Christ in you,' and I have had victory, rest and such sweet blessing ever since."

"Mystery hid from ancient ages,
But at length to faith made plain,
Christ in me, the hope of glory,
Tell it o'er and o'er again."

O BLESSED PARACLETE

O blessed Paraclete,
    Assert Thine inward sway;
My body make the temple meet,
    For Thy perpetual stay.

Too long this house of Thine
    By alien loves possessed,
Has shut from Thee its inner shrine,
    Kept Thee a slighted Guest.

Now rend, O Spirit blest,
    The veil of my poor heart;
Enter Thy long-forbidden rest,
    And nevermore depart.

Oh, to be filled with Thee!
    I ask not aught beside;
For all unholy guests must flee
    If Thou abide in me.

A. J. Gordon

8 THE FULLNESS OF THE HOLY SPIRIT

> In the last day, that great day of the feast, Jesus stood and cried, saying, If any man thirst, let him come unto me, and drink. He that believeth on me, as the scripture hath said, out of his belly shall flow rivers of living water. (But this spake he of the Spirit, which they that believe on him should receive: for the Holy Ghost was not yet given; because that Jesus was not yet glorified.
> John 7:37-39

OF THE MANY PICTURES of God's ideal of the Christian life, few are more alluring than that painted by our Lord on the last day of the Feast of Tabernacles. It was the portrayal of a life of perennial fullness and torrential overflow, to be enjoyed by all who are united to Him by faith.

These verses foreshadowed the outpouring of the Holy Spirit upon the infant Church at Pentecost, and afterward on all who believed, for, said Peter, "the promise is unto you, and to your children, and to all that are afar off, even as many as the Lord our God shall call" (Acts 2:39).

The consecration of Aaron as high priest affords an exquisitely chosen illustration of this truth. So lavishly was the holy anointing oil poured on his mitred head, that it streamed down his body, reaching even to the fringe of his priestly garments. "It is like the precious oil upon the head," said the Psalmist, "that ran down upon the beard, even Aaron's beard; that went down to the skirts of his garments" (Ps. 133:2).

Pentecost interprets this vivid symbolical act. On Christ our High Priest the Holy Spirit was poured in unmeasured fullness (John 3:34). The anointing was bestowed in such profusion that it overflowed to His mystical body, reaching to its last and least member, to the very skirts of His garments.

But today thousands of Christians live as though there had been no day of Pentecost, as though there was no share for them in the Pentecostal effusion. In this fact lies the root cause of our individual and collective powerlessness and barrenness.

"To think that I have been a Christian all these years, and I never knew until this morning that the Holy Spirit could be all this to me," the elder of a large church lamented when he listened to a sermon on this theme. Unfortunately he is not alone in his ignorance.

It was to a company of spiritually gifted Christians who had been blessed with every spiritual blessing (1:3), who had been sealed with the Spirit (1:13), who had received the earnest of the Spirit (1:14), that the categorical command came; "Be not drunk with wine wherein is excess, but *be filled with the Spirit*" (Eph. 5:18).

Wine is the devil's stimulant. The fullness of the Holy Spirit is the divine Stimulus. There is the possibility of excess in drinking wine, but not in being filled with the Spirit.

In this dual command there is both comparison and contrast. Like wine, the fullness of the Spirit produces unnatural boldness, utterance, power, optimism. The man in his cups is afraid of no one. His stammering tongue is loosed. He feels equal to anything. Failure is unthinkable. He feels exhilarated by a power entirely outside himself. And such can be the effects on a timid Christian who is filled with the Spirit.

But in contrast to wine, the Spirit's fullness results in wisdom instead of folly, self-control instead of riot, holiness instead of hellishness.

THE NATURE OF THE SPIRIT-FILLED LIFE

The Spirit-filled life is the life of a yielded believer, dominated, controlled and empowered by the Holy Spirit, even as a drunkard is dominated and controlled by his wine. It is the life of the risen Christ reproduced in the life of His child. The thirteenth chapter of Paul's first letter to the Corinthians translated into the experience of the Christian is the Spirit-filled life. It is the exemplification of the teaching of the Sermon on the Mount; it is life after the pattern seen in the Early Church.

THE PURPOSE OF THE SPIRIT-FILLED LIFE

This life is for every Christian in everyday life. It is the normal Christian life depicted ideally in the New Testament. Not reserved for a select few saintly souls, it is not for extraordinary conditions and circumstances.

A young man, who had no background of Bible knowledge, was converted. Coming to the New Testament with a virgin mind, he read the Acts of the Apostles with a bounding heart. This was life indeed. But when he came to know more intimately the body of Christians with whom he worshiped, he detected an appalling discrepancy between the apostolic pattern and present-day reality.

Was it all a mirage? he questioned. *Was such a life possible?* Judging by what he saw, he reluctantly concluded that it was not. At this crisis he was invited to attend a convention after the "Keswick" pattern. Here he was fed with "the finest of the wheat" and had fellowship with many Christians who were rejoicing in the fullness of the Holy Spirit. After some days he exclaimed, "They've got it here!" He had seen at least some approximation of the sample of Pentecost.

The fullness of the Spirit is God's provision for every relationship of life. In the verses immediately succeeding this command, the apostle details the way in which this fullness would affect life in the domestic and business spheres, for it is relevant to the whole scope of our daily lives. It is for every occupation, whether secular or sacred. It is for old and young, for male and female. In this provision, God has no favored class.

This is clear from the terms used: "all flesh"; "sons and daughters"; "young men and maidens"; "old men"; "your children"; "them that are afar off"; "as many as the Lord our God shall call." In the light of this inclusiveness, no one has any excuse for thinking that such a life is not for him. It is possible for any Christian to be "full of the Holy Spirit." It should be remembered that of the 120 present in the upper room on the day of Pentecost, there were both men and women, and most of them remained obscure Christians, serving the Lord in their ordinary vocations. Only eleven of them became apostles.

This life is for ordinary Christians in ordinary Christian service. A crisis arose in the affairs of the early church when discontent arose over the way in which relief for the needy was being administered. Some believers felt that there was discrimination and that their friends and relatives were being badly treated. Feeling that they had been called to give themselves primarily to the ministry of the Word of God and prayer, the apostles were loath to sacrifice these for the necessary though less important social ministry. Their solution of the problem has important lessons for the church of our day.

For the carrying out of even the social activities of their church-life—handling finance and caring for the needy—the local church would have only Spirit-filled men. "Wherefore, brethren, look ye out among you seven men of honest report, _full of the Holy Spirit_ and wisdom, whom we may appoint over this business" (Acts 6:3).

The fullness of the Spirit for these men was not for the working of miracles or the preaching of sermons, but to enable them to do prosaic and hidden tasks in a God-glorifying manner. The life-giving touch of the Spirit is necessary for every kind of work.

This life is for specially-called Christians for special work. There is an entirely unwarranted and un-Scriptural view promulgated in some circles, that all believers are equally called and equipped to do the work of an evangelist or teacher. But Scripture teaches differently. "And he gave some apostles, and some prophets, and some evangelists, and some pastors and teachers, for the perfecting of the saints, for the work of the ministry, for the edifying of the body of Christ" (Eph. 4:11, 12). For these ministries, those who have been specially called by God needed a special enduement of the Spirit.

Peter, in prison with John, was called upon to make a defense before the high priests of the activities of the infant church. Its whole future would be affected by the wisdom and cogency of his answer. It was no ordinary occasion. How did God equip him for this emergency for which he had no precedent?

"Then Peter, *filled with the Holy Spirit,* said unto them, Ye rulers of the people and elders of Israel, if we be examined this day of the good deed done to the impotent man . . . be it known unto you all that by the name of Jesus Christ of Nazareth whom ye crucified . . . doth this man stand before you whole. . . . Now when they saw the boldness of Peter and John . . . they marvelled; and they took knowledge of them that they had been with Jesus . . . So they let them go" (Acts 4:8-10, 13, 21).

From the tense of the verb, "filled," we learn that this was a special, sudden filling of the Holy Spirit, given to equip Peter for this special occasion.

When Paul and Barnabas set out from Antioch on their epoch-making missionary journey, the whole future of the Christian Church was in the balance. Would it remain a local sect, or would it become a world-wide religion? Much hung on the successful issue of this tour.

When the missionaries arrived at Paphos, the deputy of the area evinced a deep interest in their message. But Satan had his emissary ready to hinder the incipient work of God—Elymas the sorcerer who withstood them and "sought to turn away the deputy from the faith."

How will Paul deal with this crucial situation? "Then

95

Paul, *filled with the Holy Spirit,* set his eyes on him and said, O full of all subtlety and all mischief, thou child of the devil, thou enemy of all righteousness, wilt thou not cease to pervert the right ways of the Lord? And now behold, the hand of the Lord is upon thee, and thou shalt be blind" (Acts 13:9-11).

In these abnormal circumstances Paul, as the tense of the verb again suggests, experienced a special filling of the Spirit to empower him to deal with Satanic opposition. The filling in this sense is spasmodic, received as and when the need arises. For every unusual demand, God has a special enduement. Whenever we are called upon to exercise some special or critical ministry, there will be a special equipment of power or grace awaiting us.

This life is for fruitfulness for every Christian. Fruit is the overflowing of life. The abundant life of the root expresses itself in fruit on the branch. On the part of the branch, the bearing of fruit is entirely unconscious and effortless. All it needs to do is to maintain unbroken union with the root. So with the Christian.

"I have chosen and ordained you," said the Lord to His disciples, "that ye should go and bring forth fruit, and that your fruit should remain" (John 15:16).

THE EFFECTS OF THE SPIRIT'S FILLING

One of the outstanding transformations in the lives of the apostles after Pentecost was their *boldness in witness-bearing.* Immediately upon being filled with the Spirit, Peter the coward became Peter the courageous. The other disciples, all of whom had forsaken Jesus and fled when He was arrested and who even ten days before Pentecost were hiding behind barred doors for fear of the Jews, were suddenly transformed.

"Ye shall be witnesses unto me," Jesus had said to them. "And *they were all filled with the Holy Spirit,* and they spoke the word of God with boldness," was the fulfillment (Acts 1:8; 4:31). I remember a timid girl, too shy to converse much on ordinary topics. After

96

yielding her life to the Lord and being filled with the Spirit, she became as bold as a lion when witnessing to her ungodly workmates. She had claimed her birthright, and the Holy Spirit enabled her to witness with boldness.

But the fullness of the Spirit results in *power in witness bearing,* as well as boldness. "Ye shall receive *power* when the Holy Spirit is come upon you, and ye shall be my witnesses," was the promise. "And with great *power* gave the apostles their witness," was the fulfillment (Acts 1:8, RV; 4:33, RV).

If all preachers enjoyed the Spirit's fullness, there would not be so much powerless and ineffective preaching. When the Lord called His disciples to undertake the superhuman task of world-wide witness, He endued them with the supernatural power of the Holy Spirit, for wherever the Spirit is in fullness, He manifests Himself in power. "My preaching was in demonstration of the Spirit and of *power"* was Paul's testimony (1 Cor. 2:4).

After his Pentecostal experience, Peter's sermon was liquid logic delivered with flaming eloquence. And it achieved its objective. "They were pricked to the heart and said, Men and brethren, what shall we do?" The effect of the sermon by the Spirit-filled Stephen was that "they were not able to resist the wisdom and the spirit by which he spoke" (Acts 6:10). "They were cut to the heart." There was no mouthing of pious platitudes, no ineffectiveness here.

At a crisis in his spiritual experience, Jonathan Goforth of Korea, a noted missionary and revivalist, gave himself to the detailed study of the teaching of the Scriptures on the Holy Spirit. He rose early to get uninterrupted time with his Bible. Fearing he would break down, his wife said to him, "Jonathan, are you not going too far in this?" Rising from his knees he faced her with a look she never forgot. "Oh, Rose, even you do not understand! I feel like one who has tapped a mine of wealth. It is so wonderful. Oh, if I could only get others to see it!"

What was the result of the unprecedented filling of the Spirit which he had received?

One night while speaking to a heathen audience which filled the street chapel, Goforth witnessed a stirring among the people which he had never seen before. As he was speaking on the verse, "He bore our sins in his own body on the tree," conviction of sin was written on every face. When he asked for decisions, practically everyone responded. During the days that followed, at every center where he peached the Gospel, men came seeking salvation.

The Spirit's fullness *fits for suffering and sacrifice*. Those who associate the experience only with ecstatic emotional experiences and great revivals, should read other portions of Scripture such as these:

"Stephen, *full of the Holy Spirit* said, Behold, I see the heavens opened, and the Son of man standing on the right hand of God . . . . and they ran upon him with one accord, and cast him out of the city. And they stoned Stephen . . . . And he cried with a loud voice, Lord, lay not this sin to their charge" (Acts 7: 55-60).

"The Lord said to Ananias . . . He is a chosen vessel unto me . . . I will show him [Paul] how great things he must suffer for my sake . . . And Ananias said, Brother Saul the Lord hath sent me . . . . that thou mightest be *filled with the Holy Spirit*."

Note in both cases the intimate connection between the suffering and the filling. Who suffered so greatly as the Spirit-filled Paul? It is possible to glorify God as much in the fires of suffering as in the floods of revival.

THE CONDITIONS OF BEING SPIRIT-FILLED

There is no such thing as "Three easy steps into the Spirit-filled life," for it involves ruthless honesty with ourselves, and radical dealing with everything that would grieve the Holy Spirit. And yet, if we are prepared for any cost involved, the conditions are not complex. A study of the relevant Scriptures would seem to indicate these four steps into the experience.

1. *Acknowledge.* If what has been written before has made it clear that you have not been living a Spirit-filled life, that you are not filled with the Spirit, honestly acknowledge the fact. Put it into words in the Lord's presence. If you have tolerated sin in your life, acknowledge that too, and put it away forever. Right things must be kept in their right place. Doubtful things must be surrendered. Wrong things must be abandoned. If this is done sincerely, we can claim the cleansing promised to those who confess their sins (1 John 1:9).

2. *Ask.* Since to be filled with the Spirit is something which God has commanded, we can ask confidently and importunately that we may know this experience. "If ye then being evil, know how to give good gifts unto your children, how much more will your heavenly Father give the Holy Spirit to them that *ask* him" (Luke 11:13). *"Ask* and ye shall receive."

In asking thus, we are not requesting God to give us the Holy Spirit as a Person, for He has already given Him to the whole Church. The meaning here, borne out by the grammatical construction, is that God will give Him to us in the unhindered exercise of all His powers and attributes.

3. *Abdicate.* If Christ has not been enthroned in our hearts as Lord and King, then the throne is still occupied by the usurper Self. The Holy Spirit's fullness is known only by those who recognize the Lordship of Christ, who abdicate the throne of their lives in His favor.

When Peter was told in vision to eat of the things contained in the sheet let down from heaven (Acts 10:14), his reply was, "Not so, Lord." Peter was unconscious of the incongruity, indeed the impossibility of his statement. If Christ was his Lord in reality, then he could never say, "Not so," to Him. To do so would be tantamount to denying His Lordship. We modern Peters may call Him Lord, but how often we have said in effect, "Not so, Lord," when He has moved us to pray in a prayer meeting, or to witness to someone about Him; when He has urged us to break with some sin or yield some doubtful thing; when He has called on us to make restitution of money or send a letter of apology; when He has called us to missionary service; when He has moved us to give sacrificially. The words on the lips of the Spirit-filled Christian are never, "Not so, Lord," but always, "Master and Lord."

4. *Accept*. It is not sufficient merely to ask; we must accept by an act of faith what God has promised and we have asked. How were the Galatians to receive this blessing? "That we might receive the promise of the Spirit *through faith*" (Gal. 3:14) was Paul's explanation. When we honestly comply with God's conditions we may confidently count on His fulfilling His promise, as He did on the day of Pentecost (Acts 1:8; 2:4).

> I simply take Him at His word,
> I praise Him that my prayer is heard,
> And claim my answer from the Lord,
> I take, He undertakes.

THE SPIRIT-FILLED LIFE

O the Spirit-filled life; is it thine, is it thine?
Is thy soul wholly filled with the Spirit Divine?
O thou child of the King, has He fallen on thee?
Does He reign in thy soul, so that all men may see
The dear Savior's blest image reflected in thee?

Has He swept thro' thy soul like the waves of the sea?
Does the Spirit of God daily rest upon thee?
Does He sweeten thy life, does He keep thee from care?
Does He guide thee and bless thee in answer to prayer?
Is it joy to be led of the Lord anywhere?

Has He purged thee of dross with the fire from above?
Is He first in thy thoughts, has He all of thy love?
Is His service thy choice, and is sacrifice sweet?
Is the doing His will both thy drink and thy meat?
Dost thou run at His bidding with eager glad feet?

Has He freed thee from self, and from all of thy greed?
Dost thou hasten to succor thy brother in need?
As a soldier of Christ dost thou hardness endure?
Is thy hope in the Lord everlasting and sure?
Hast thou patience and meekness, art tender and pure?

O, the Spirit-filled life may be thine, may be thine,
In thy soul evermore the Shekinah may shine;
It is thine to live with the tempests all stilled,
It is thine with the blessed Holy Ghost to be filled;
It is thine, even thine, for thy Lord has so willed.

9 EVIDENCES OF THE SPIRIT'S FULLNESS

Reading: Ephesians 5:18–6:9*

ONE OF THE CHARACTERISTIC features of the early church was that being filled with the Spirit was the norm for its members. The men chosen to be responsible even for the "social work" of the church must be men "full of the Holy Spirit."

In the previous study we saw that the Spirit-filled life is one in which the Holy Spirit is granted absolute control of the human personality. This makes it possible for Him to endue the believer with power for spiritual service, and to produce in him His ninefold fruit.

A careful reading of the relevant Scriptures reveals that the evidences of the Spirit's fullness in any life do not consist in emotional states, in ecstatic utterances, or in signs and visions, but in certain practical effects in character, relationships and service.

These evidences are readily discernible to the observer, and are not liable to counterfeit, as are the more subjective manifestations. Nor do they revolve around and minister to the selfish enjoyment of the believer. Their object is to glorify Christ in the details of life and service, and to strengthen and help others. It is essentially an outgoing and outflowing life; and in the passage for our study, its effects on normal human relationships are demonstrated—

IN PERSONAL LIFE (Eph. 5:18-20).

The character of our conversation is the first evidence: "Speaking out your thoughts to each other in

---

* Because of the length of this and subsequent readings, the reader is requested to read the passage indicated in his own Bible.

103

psalms, in hymns, in chants inspired by the Spirit" (v. 19, Way).

Does our conversation match this exhortation? From the context it is clear that this should be the natural expression of being filled with the Spirit. Conversation will be spiritual and Christo-centric. This does not mean that topics of everyday concern will not be discussed, but it does mean that it will be natural to turn conversation into spiritual channels when that is appropriate and possible.

It is challenging to reflect on the fact that we have often been more ready to speak of other things than about Him. We often discuss the failings of our fellows, our Christian work, our business, our children, our ailments, but find ourselves strangely reluctant to speak of Him. As all roads lead to Rome, so should our conversation lead naturally to Christ. If we are filled with the Spirit who is the supreme Lover of Christ, we will find Him drawing our thoughts and conversation to Him, as the lodestone draws the needle to itself.

The presence of song in the life will be another evidence of the Spirit's fullness. "Let the sound of your singing, let the music of your hearts go up to the Lord" (v. 19, Way). Bursts of song from a happy heart will replace grumbling and complaining. Song is an index of the condition of the inner man. "You can always tell when Grandpa gets up," said his daughter, "because the moment his feet hit the floor he starts to sing." A heart in fellowship with God and filled with the Spirit finds expression in spontaneous song.

We never sing when we are miserable. Many a husband or wife would be dumbfounded if their partner spontaneously burst into a song of praise, and yet should it be unusual? Not all of us have melodious voices, but it is as acceptable to God to "make melody in your heart unto the Lord" as to express your joy vocally.

The Rev. G. C. Grubb used to be accompanied in his evangelistic campaigns by a Tamil Christian with a radiant countenance and an equally radiant testimony. He used to say that he had a music box in his heart and couldn't help singing. Many were drawn to Christ initially by this man's spontaneous song.

There is unexploited power in the uninhibited singing of the great hymns of the church. In recognition of this, singing is accorded an important role in both Old and New Testament times in the worship of God's people. "When they began to sing and to praise, the Lord set ambushments against the enemy," the record runs.

The practice of giving thanks in all things is a third evidence. "Giving thanks always for all things unto God and the Father in the name of our Lord Jesus Christ" (v. 20).

This evidence of the fullness of the Spirit is to be taken in all its literal absoluteness. "Always"; "for all things." It is not for us to do away with the implication of this exhortation, simply because of its incredibly high demand. To the Spirit-filled believer there are no second causes. Since everything that touches his life comes by direct permission of God, he can always thank his Father, even if it be in blind faith.

A. S. Way translates this sentence, "In increasing thanksgiving for all that he sends you." But this is not always our attitude. We take so much from Him and others as if it were only our due. We often give Him cause to say, "Were there not ten cleansed? But where are the nine?"

When the Holy Spirit has full control of us, a spirit of thanksgiving for anything and everything will characterize us. In our prayer-life, giving of thanks will be a regular spiritual exercise.

Judging our personal lives by these divine standards, can we say that we are filled with God's Spirit?

Before embarking on details of the domestic scene Paul intimates that the Spirit-filled life is a life of mutual submission rather than of individual self-assertion. "Submitting yourselves one to another in the fear of God" (v. 21). It would seem that this should apply to Christian relationships in general, and not only to the marital relationship.

Church councils and committee meetings would get further and achieve more if this quality of submission was more in evidence. While there is room for firmness where matters of major principle are involved, there are many occasions when mutual submission would open the way to a speedy solution of a thorny problem. It has rightly been said that often when we think we are standing for principle, we are only falling for prejudice.

The Christian home is the citadel of Christianity. Guided by the Holy Spirit, the apostle proceeds to show how Spirit-filled believers will deport themselves in the exacting relationships of marital and domestic life.

The first exhortation is addressed to *wives*. "Wives, yield submission to your lawful husbands; do it as service to our Lord" (v. 22, Way).

This sounds strangely out of keeping with modern trends and yet these are the words, not merely of Paul the apostle, but of the Holy Spirit under whose inspiration they were written. Read by itself, the injunction may seem sweeping and unfair, but taken in its context, and read in conjunction with the even more stringent exhortations to husbands, it is not as unreasonable as it may at first appear.

It is not a question of the superiority of the husband and the inferiority of the wife, for no such idea is involved. It has to do with the respective positions which God in His love and wisdom has assigned to each.

The submission of the wife to her husband is to be

106

"as unto the Lord, for the husband *is* the head of the wife, even as the Lord *is* the head of the church" (v. 23). The Spirit-filled wife accepts the position assigned to her by God, and is subject to her husband, "as the church is subject to Christ" (v. 24). She is to "reverence," or better, "respect" her husband (v. 33). The ideally happy marriage is where both wife and husband are Spirit-filled, and in their relationships, obey the divine exhortations. Where the positions of husband and wife in the home are reversed, conditions are likely to be far from ideal. If it is no dishonor to the church to be subject to Christ, then it is no dishonor to the wife to be subject to her husband.

If God expects a geat deal of wives, He expects even more of husbands. "Husbands, love your wives even as Christ also loved the church and gave himself for it" (v. 25). "So ought men to love their wives as their own bodies" (v. 28). "Let every one of you so love his wife even as himself" (v. 33).

If all husbands conformed to this standard, wives would experience little difficulty in being subject to them. The Holy Spirit in these exhortations recognizes that if wives were in danger of failing to be subject to their husbands, there is an equal danger that husbands will not love their wives sacrificially and unselfishly. The standard established for a husband's love for his wife, is that of Christ's love for His Church. We may well take Paul's words on our lips, "Who is sufficient for these things?" The answer is, "Be filled with the Spirit," and He will make you sufficient.

If a love such as this, flowing from the Spirit of love, characterized husbands, there would be fewer sad and disappointed wives in the world. Homes are often robbed of harmony and happiness by the thoughtlessness and selfishness of the husband. The greatest element in Christ's love for His Church was its utter unselfishness — sacrifice even to death. The Spirit-filled husband, in the most intimate relationships with his wife will be characterized by unselfish love.

Even *children* may know what it is to be filled with the Spirit, for it is no merely adult privilege. The apostle indicates how this will be evidenced in their lives: "Children, obey your parents in the Lord . . . . Honor thy father and thy mother" (6:1-2).

Disobedience to parents and failing to honor them is no modern phenomenon, but it would be no exaggeration to say that in our day this attitude has reached epidemic proportions. The evidence that a teenager is filled with the Spirit will be seen, not so much in a thrilling experience or tide of emotion, as in honoring and obeying his father and mother.

Paul was not unsympathetic to the peculiar problems and temptations of youth, so he counseled: "Ye fathers, provoke not your children to wrath, but bring them up in the nurture and admonition of the Lord" (6:4). In other words, fathers are to be reasonable with their children, not expecting adult reactions from them and they are to make it as easy as possible for their children to be obedient. Bringing up children "in the nurture and admonition of the Lord" will certainly include maintaining family worship, and a high standard of personal life on the part of parents.

Wives, husbands, fathers, children can judge whether or not they are filled with the Spirit by these very practical evidences.

IN BUSINESS LIFE (Eph. 6:5-9)

Scripture gives no countenance to the idea that "Jack is as good as his master," and can therefore act as he pleases in a business relationship. The mutual responsibilities of master and servant are here recognized and defined. To understand the full significance of this passage it should be remembered that at the time it was written, almost half the people in the Roman Empire were slaves. In the church many were slaves, and it would be easy for them, because of their new freedom in Christ, to take undue liberties in their relationship with their masters. It is illuminating to notice how duty and responsibility are balanced in this passage.

"*Servants,* be obedient to them that are your masters . . . in singleness of your heart, as unto Christ, not with eyeservice as men-pleasers, but as the servants of Christ, doing the will of God from the heart . . . . as to the Lord, and not to men" (vv. 5-7).

This is a hard saying, for it applies to the bad as well as to the good master. But the indwelling Holy Spirit will make it possible. No provision is made for slothful, grudging, unwilling service. Servants are to give their service "from the heart," with good-will.

But the Holy Spirit makes equal demands on masters and mistresses. "And ye *masters,* do the same things unto them, forbearing threatening, knowing that your Master also is in heaven and there is no respect of persons with him" (v. 9).

The same Holy Spirit who will enable the servant to render glad and willing service to the master, will enable the master to show a similar spirit of consideration to his servant. He will not domineer and threaten, but while maintaining his rightful authority, he will be thoughtful and considerate. The observance of these attitudes in the realm of business would provide the solution to all labor problems. Between masters and servants such as these, no point of contention would arise.

In our relations as master and servant, do we evidence the fullness of the Spirit?

In Christian Experience

The experience of the fullness of the Spirit, as we have seen, results in a new adjustment of relationships which evidences *to others* that we are filled. But there are some evidences which can bring a similar assurance *to ourselves.*

A new consciousness of Christ's indwelling presence is the first. The Holy Spirit is designated *the Spirit of Christ,* and He makes Christ the home of our

109

thoughts and the center of our affections. "At that day ye shall know that I am in my Father, and ye in me, and *I in you,*" was our Lord's promise, and the Holy Spirit makes it real in the experience of the believer whom He fills.

A new likeness to Christ's holy character is another evidence. Ungrieved by tolerated sin or disobedience, *the Spirit of Holiness* produces His fruit in luxuriant measure (Gal. 5:22, 23). This was evidenced in the changed lives of the disciples after their Pentecostal experience when "they were all filled with the Holy Spirit." Love that passes knowledge, joy unspeakable and full of glory, peace that passes all understanding became their experience. In their conduct, they were characterized by longsuffering, gentleness and goodness. In their characters they displayed faithfulness, meekness and self-control. What the Spirit did in them, He can do in us.

A new experience of Christ's supernatural power became theirs. Their witness was in demonstration of the Spirit and of power, because they were filled with *the Spirit of power.* To those He fills He imparts power to suffer and sacrifice as well as to witness and work.

If these characteristics are present in our lives, we can know that the Holy Spirit fills and controls us.

MY HOLY GUEST

Holy Ghost, I bid Thee welcome,
  Come and be my Holy Guest;
Heav'nly Dove within my bosom,
  Make Thy home and build Thy nest.

I am lone and sad without Thee,
  Thou hast made my heart for Thee;
Leave me not a helpless orphan,
  Come, oh come and dwell with me.

Come and banish all that grieves Thee,
  Come and cleanse from all my sin;
Bring me Jesus in all fullness,
  Make my heart a heav'n within.

Lead me on to all Thy fullness,
  Bring me to Thy promised rest;
Holy Ghost I bid Thee welcome,
  Be my Holy, heavenly Guest.

A. B. Simpson

10 THE PARTNERSHIP OF THE HOLY SPIRIT

> The grace of our Lord Jesus Christ, and the love of God, and the communion of the Holy Ghost be with you all. 2 Corinthians 13:14

THE BUSINESS OF LIVING the Christian life as it is set forth in the New Testament, is too exacting in its standards, too lofty in its ideals for us to achieve by ourselves. We need a partner with adequate capital and ability.

In our daily papers, an advertisement such as this is often seen: "Wanted, a partner, with capital, to develop a promising business." The advertiser has the business, but is hampered in the development of its potential by a lack of capital, hence the advertisement.

We find ourselves in a somewhat analogous position in our Christian lives. We have embarked on the business of Christian living, but have already discovered how hopelessly inadequate is our spiritual capital. As we read the New Testament we come upon exhortations and commands such as these:

"Be ye therefore perfect, even as your Father in heaven is perfect" (Matt. 5:48).
"Be ye holy, for I am holy" (1 Pet. 1:16).
"In nothing be anxious" (Phil. 4:6).
"Always giving thanks for all things" (Eph. 5:20).
"Pray without ceasing" (1 Thess. 5:17).

But how can we hope to attain a standard such as this? How scale these heights of spiritual attainment? Such a life may be for spiritual giants, but not for ordinary run-of-the-mill people like ourselves.

Our heavenly Father would not be God if He asked of us something impossible of attainment. No human father would tease and discourage his son by doing such a thing. The fact is that all God's commands are enablings. Augustine had the key when he prayed, "O God, give what Thou commandest, then command what Thou wilt." God has made provision for our attaining all that He commands.

What we need is a Partner who can share this business of Christian living with us, a Partner who has the "know-how" and adequate resources at his disposal. Here, as everywhere, we find in the Godhead, the complement of every spiritual need. In this case, it is what Paul calls "the communion [partnership] of the Holy Spirit" (2 Cor. 3:14).

We have heard the words of this benediction hundreds of times, but we may never have apprehended the possibilities implicit in the words, "the communion [or fellowship] of the Holy Spirit." The word "communion" signifies the sharing of something. In Acts 4:32 it refers to the sharing of goods. In 1 John 1:3 it refers to fellowship shared with God. In Luke 5:7 it signifies *partnership in business*. Five times in the New Testament it is translated "partner," so the suggestion that the Holy Spirit is our Partner is entirely in keeping with the tenor of Scripture.

THE PERSONALITY OF THE PARTNER

Most of you who read these lines will probably believe and accept the doctrine of the personality of the Holy Spirit. Most would refer to the Spirit as Him, not it, for they recognize that He is not a force or influence or power, but a divine Person. We recognize His personality as an item of doctrine, but do we recognize it as a matter of fact in our experience? In what way do we honor His personality? Do we think of Him as a living Person, just as real, as loving, as Christ Himself? Is it not true that with many of us He does not enter into our thinking or our lives in any meaningful way? Yet without His many-sided ministry, our spiritual lives would soon be bankrupt.

When speaking to His disciples of the coming of the

114

Comforter, our Lord uttered four pregnant words which challenge us all. The words are, *"But ye know him"* (John 14:17). Know whom? The Holy Spirit. We could assuredly answer affirmatively if this assertion were made of God the Father or of Jesus Christ the Son, but can we say that in any similar manner we *know* the Holy Spirit as a divine Person? We know God as a loving Father. We know Jesus as a Savior and Friend. But do we in a similar sense know the Holy Spirit, the Third Person of the Trinity as our Indwelling Comforter and Enduer?

If we are to prosper spiritually, we must remember that we are not utilizing an influence or power, but we have a personal relationship with a divine, personal Partner, One with whom we can have intimate fellowship. Can we in any real sense enjoy the partnership of the Holy Spirit if we do not *know* Him as One worthy of equal honor, love and worship with the Father and the Son?

The Purpose of the Partnership

If there is to be harmony and success in a partnership, it is of utmost importance that both partners be as one in their business aims and ideals. Even though both may be thoroughly upright, the relationship may become unhappy and galling if the partners cherish divergent interests and ideals.

The Holy Spirit was sent to earth to transact big business for the Heavenly House He represents—nothing less than the redemption of a lost world. In this enterprise He seeks our partnership. He is Christ's Advocate on earth, overseeing and advancing His interests. His chief concern is *the furthering of the glory of Christ among men.* This is the purpose of the partnership, and this is to be the supreme objective of our life and service.

"He shall glorify me," was our Lord's summary of the ministry of the Paraclete. If we are in true partnership with Him, we will do the same. In so far as this is the case, we can count on the fullest cooperation of our Partner, whether our sphere of service is pulpit or factory, mission field or home.

> Spirit of Jesus, glorify
>   The Master's name in me;
> Whether I live, or if I die,
>   Let Christ exalted be.

THE POSITION OF THE PARTNERS

Some businesses function quite successfully with one "working" partner and one "silent" partner. The latter, though not taking any part in the actual conduct of the partnership's affairs, provides the necessary capital and participates in the profits.

But the Holy Spirit will be party to no such arrangement. *He must be Senior and Controlling Partner*. His Personality must dominate our personalities. May it not be that our comparative ineffectiveness in service has its source here? We have arrogated to ourselves the role of senior partner, and assigned to the Holy Spirit that of silent Partner. We have been making use of Him instead of permitting Him to make use of us.

The story of Gideon affords a striking illustration of the correct relationship between the Holy Spirit and the Christian. "The Spirit of the Lord clothed himself with Gideon" (Judg. 6:34, margin). Using Gideon as His clothing, the Spirit of God achieved through him a great victory over Israel's foes. Gideon became a powerful instrument in the hand of God because He recognized the relative positions of himself and the Spirit of God.

One day as the American evangelist, Dwight L. Moody, was walking with his wife by the Syrian Sea, he told her of an aged man who had greatly annoyed him by saying, "Young man, honor thou the Holy Spirit, or thou shalt break down!"

"I was angry," said Moody, "but he was right. My heart was troubled, and I prayed, prayed until there

came the night when the Third Heaven found me . . . .
Since then my soul has known the mystery of Moses'
bush which burned with fire, but was not consumed."

If we honor the Holy Spirit and accord to Him the
position of Senior Partner, it will mean that what seems
good to Him will seem good to us also (Acts 15:28).
We will embark on no enterprises which He has not
initiated, or concerning which we have not first secured
His approval. He will always be consulted and His
counsel followed. The last word will always be with
Him, for He is the Senior Partner.

THE TERMS OF THE PARTNERSHIP

For a successful and harmonious partnership, it is
essential to have the terms defined to the last particular,
and agreed upon by both parties. He is unwise who
enters into a partnership even with a friend, without
having these terms embodied in a partnership deed.

The normal partnership agreement embodies at least
the following conditions:

*The business shall be conducted according to the
partnership deed.* Our partnership deed is the Spirit-
breathed Word of God. In it is contained in principle,
guidance for every contingency which can possibly arise
in the course of our business for God. It is important,
therefore, that we acquaint ourselves with *all* the pro-
visions of the partnership deed, and conform our lives
to its demands.

*The partners shall devote their whole time, ability
and energies to the furthering of their joint business.*
There is no question of the Holy Spirit failing to fulfill His responsibilities in the partnership. He will not
only do His own share, but He will empower us also
in our work of glorifying Christ in the salvation of
souls and building up His Church. This is implicit in
our Lord's promise, "Ye shall receive power, the Holy
Spirit coming upon you, and ye shall be witnesses unto
me" (Acts 1:8).

As did our Master, we will be willing to sacrifice

117

personal interests and comforts in the interests of His Kingdom. We will enter into no alliances with those in the opposition business—the world, the flesh and the devil.

The capital to be contributed. What can we contribute to the partnership in the way of capital? We have nothing which we have not received. But we do have something of great value in the estimation of our heavenly Partner — our redeemed lives and personalities, with all their powers and possibilities. Though the gift is so poor—and we know that better than anyone else—we are "in His image," and therefore acceptable to the Holy Spirit.

What is the contribution of the Senior Partner to the partnership assets? "The unsearchable riches of Christ" in whom are hid "all the treasures of wisdom and knowledge" — capital enough, surely, for all our need.

W. Y. Fullerton told of a young man who, to the astonishment of his friends, launched out into a large business. They could not understand how a young man with little capital was able to attempt so much. The factor of which they were unaware was that a wealthy businessman, discerning the young man's business acumen, had said to him, "You begin, and I will stand by you. If you want advice or advances, come to me." It was this hidden stand-by who enabled him to achieve what otherwise would have been impossible.

In our partnership business, we too have an unseen "Stand-by" who is always willing and able to give advice or make advances as the need arises. We can therefore, in faith attempt service for God far beyond our own resources or natural ability. What we lack, our Partner will supply. We can never overdraw our spiritual capital, for God "hath blessed us with all spiritual blessings . . . in Christ" (Eph. 1:3).

In the event of any disagreement or dispute arising, the matter shall be referred to an arbitrator. Who will be the arbitrator if the partnership arrangements break down? Provision is made for this in the partnership deed. "May the peace of Christ be throned in your heart as the arbitrator in all disputes" (Col. 3:15, Way).

If the dove of peace has flown from our hearts, we can know at once that we are not in harmony with our Senior Partner. We have grieved the Holy Spirit. Honest and sincere confession and forsaking of the sin which ruptured the relationship, and the renewal of obedience and full cooperation, will secure the return of the dove of peace.

The distribution of profits. It will be seen that in this partnership, we are given the best of the bargain, but nowhere more than in this respect. Unlike most partners, the Holy Spirit seeks nothing for Himself. All the profits which accrue as a result of the partnership business, He makes over to us, in spite of our paltry contribution to the capital. He constitutes us "heirs of God, and joint-heirs with our Lord Jesus Christ," and all that He has becomes ours. What amazing magnanimity this is!

THE PRIVILEGES OF THE PARTNERSHIP

This partnership with the Holy Spirit confers on us unique privileges:

In the study of the Bible. As the Spirit of truth, the inspirer and interpreter of the Scriptures, He makes available to us His gracious help. As we traverse the Scriptures in fellowship with Him, He illumines its pages, reveals its secrets, and portrays the glory of God in the face of Jesus Christ. In spiritual conflicts we can count on Him whose sword is the Word of God.

In the secret place of prayer. Our Partner has delight in helping us in our communion with heaven. We can often account for our barrenness in prayer by our failure to be in fellowship with our Partner who is "the *Spirit of Prayer.*" He is able to help us in both the infirmities of our bodies and the ignorance of our

119

minds in the ministry of prayer (Rom. 8:26). Let us not forget our Partner in our prayer-life.

In our service for Christ. As we endeavor in Christian service to glorify Christ, the Spirit delights to come to our aid. We can turn to Him not only for advice but also for power and effectiveness. For is He not "the *Spirit of Power*"?

In daily life. It would be impossible for us to be long associated with *"the Spirit of holiness,"* without partaking in some measure of His characteristic quality, for He conducts His operations, not from without, but from within. He is "the Holy Spirit that dwelleth in you." As He is holy, He will make us increasingly holy as we are more and more conformed to the image of Christ. As He is gracious, He will make us gracious. As He is the Spirit of truth, He will make us truthful. As He is loving, He will make us loving.

The benediction with which we have so long been familiar, should have a deeper significance when we realize more of what is involved in the phrase, "The partnership of the Holy Spirit."

Part Two

THE CONQUEST OF CANAAN

A series of Bible studies drawing contemporary spiritual lessons from Israel's trek from the Wilderness to the Promised Land.

KADESH-BARNEA

They came to the gates of Canaan,
  But they never entered in;
They came to the very threshold,
  But they perished in their sin.

On the morrow they would have entered,
  But God had shut the gate.
They wept, they rashly ventured,
  But alas! it was too late.

And so we are ever coming
  To the place where two ways part,
One leads to the Land of Promise,
  And one to a hardened heart.

Oh, brother, give heed to the warning,
  And obey His voice today;
The Spirit to thee is calling,
  Oh, do not grieve Him away.

Oh, come in complete surrender,
  Oh, turn from thy doubt and sin;
Pass on from Kadesh to Canaan,
  And a crown and kingdom win.

R. Kelso Carter

11 THE TRAGEDY OF KADESH-BARNEA

*Reading: Numbers 13:26–14:34 **

Introductory Note

THE HISTORY OF ISRAEL was typical history, and of all the instructive incidents recorded, the story of their travels from Egypt to Canaan, the Land of Promise, is the most illuminating. It is replete with illuminating parallels to the experience of the Christian in his progression from the natural state, through the carnal to the spiritual plane (cf. 2 Cor. 2:14, 15; 3:1).

That this was the intention of the Inspiring Spirit is plain from the writings of Paul, and those of the author of the letter to the Hebrews (see Heb. 3:17-19; 4:1, 11). Paul does not hesitate to deduce spiritual lessons from the experiences of the Israelites:

> "Now these things were our examples [or figures], to the intent that we should not lust after evil things, as they also lusted. . . . Now all these things happened unto them for ensamples [or types]: and they are written for our admonition . . ." (1 Cor. 10:6, 11).

Thus twice over Paul assures us that more than a historical narrative is in view. In this connection, H. L. Goudge wrote in the Westminster Commentary: "We can hardly doubt that Paul regarded these Old Testament incidents as not merely valuable illustrations, but as pre-arranged types of Christian mysteries. (Cf. our Lord's words in John 6:32; 7:37ff., and Peter's application to the incident of the flood, 1 Pet. 3:20, 21.) Such views may appear fanciful to the modern mind,

---

* The reader is referred to his own Bible for the text of this lengthy Scripture passage.

but deeper knowledge of the Scripture will probably convince of their truth . . . .

"That real events, ordered by God's providence, should foreshadow the blessings to be afterwards bestowed, is far more natural than that casual and legendary narratives should do so . . . .

"If God's dealings with Israel had a special purpose which His dealings with other nations had not, a true narrative of these dealings will of necessity have a specially didactic character."

This extended note is written to indicate that there is Scriptural warrant for spiritualizing this memorable trek, and that in doing so we are following the excellent example of Paul the apostle.

The first point to be settled if these studies are to be meaningful is

THE SIGNIFICANCE OF CANAAN

God made a gift of the Land of Promise, Canaan, to Abraham almost immediately after calling him to leave home and kindred, in these words: "All the land which thou seest, to thee will I give it, and to thy seed for ever" (Gen. 13:15). Although in his lifetime Abraham never possessed more of it than would make a sepulcher, yet it became his in reality from the moment of the gift. But five hundred years elapsed before God was able to bring his descendants to the place where they possessed their possessions.

He had led them out of Egypt by signs and wonders, and brought them safely through the Red Sea and into the wilderness of Shur. From there they journeyed to Kadesh-Barnea, one of the few gateways into Canaan. At last they were actually within sight of their Promised Land.

Both hymnology and general usage have conspired to convey the impression that the River Jordan represents physical death, and Canaan, the blessedness of heaven. This is true only in a very secondary sense.

The primary significance of Canaan is not heaven,

but what Paul calls "life in the heavenlies," while still living on earth. This is the teaching of the Ephesian letter, the New Testament counterpart of the book of Joshua. Not heaven, but a suburb of heaven. *Canaan stands for a victorious type of Christian experience, possible here and now,* when the believer exchanges the defeat of the wilderness for the joy, rest and fruitfulness of the Canaan life.

That Canaan cannot represent heaven is clear on several counts. There are no battles to fight in heaven. There were in Canaan. Canaan was one prolonged battle. There is no sin in heaven, but there was sin in Canaan. There will be no defeats in heaven. There were in Canaan. Believers commit no sin in not entering heaven at once, but upon reaching Kadesh-barnea, Israel committed one long sin in refusing to enter the land.

In New Testament language, Canaan stands for a change in Christian experience as clear and definite as that which transformed the motley crowd of Hebrew slaves into a victorious army. The prospect of life in Canaan should have seemed alluring to the homeless and hapless people — a God-given land flowing with milk and honey. Possession of Canaan would mean to them:

Liberty instead of oppression. Who but a slave can appreciate the full meaning of liberty? All that Canaan must have meant in prospect to this nation of slaves, is what God promises to the believer who is still enslaved by his sin—"Sin shall not have dominion over you . . . Being then made free from sin, ye became the servants of righteousness" (Rom. 6:14, 18).

Rest instead of wandering. At long last they would have a home they could call their own. No more aimless wandering over the glaring sands. So for the believer, "there remaineth a rest . . . We which have believed do enter into rest" (Heb. 4:3, 9).

Possession instead of promise. The promise to Abraham which for centuries had remained unfulfilled was now within reach of fulfillment. They had only to take the step of faith. So for the believer who enters his Canaan, promises are turned into facts and doctrine into experience. According to his faith it is unto him.

Variety instead of monotony. In spite of their complaining, God never allowed Israel to suffer want, even in the wilderness. Never once did the manna cease or the water fail, but the monotony of the fare caused them to murmur, and to lust after the delicacies Egypt could supply. "Our soul loatheth this light bread," they complained. But life in the wilderness could not compare with that of Canaan for variety and abundance — milk and honey, corn and grapes, and much else besides. A similar abundance and variety in spiritual fare awaits the believer in his Canaan-life.

Everything is in the superlative degree—"*love* that passeth knowledge"; "*joy* unspeakable and full of glory"; *peace* that passeth all understanding." Such is the alluring prospect before him.

THE LEGITIMATE WILDERNESS EXPERIENCE

In some circles it is common to speak of our life on earth as a "wilderness experience." This may be true in a symbolical sense, but the statement needs to be greatly qualified. Compared with our future experience with Christ in heaven, life here is indeed a wilderness, but that is not the teaching of this epic journey from Kadesh to Canaan, for Canaan is not heaven.

In addition, we must distinguish between a wilderness experience which is legitimate, and one which is illegitimate, because the Israelites experienced both.

For Israel, the initial journey from the Red Sea to Kadesh-barnea was necessary, legitimate and proper, and finds its counterpart in the experience of the young convert. Now redeemed and delivered from the slavery of Satan, the new believer has yet to learn how to walk through life—through its bitter experiences, as at Marah and its sweet experiences, as at Elim. He must now rely on God for daily supplies and the maintenance of his spiritual life. It was an infinitely better experience than that of Egypt, but came far short of the delights of Canaan.

From the national point of view, the nation had been born, but it was yet in a state of spiritual infancy, not yet fit for the exacting warfare that lay ahead in Canaan. The hardships of the wilderness were designed to supply this fitness. The nation fed on bread from heaven, but sometimes longed for Egypt's dainties. They sang their joyous song of deliverance at the Red Sea, but ere long it died, and they began to complain at their lot. They leaned too heavily on human props. When Moses' masterful presence was removed for a brief period, they persuaded weak Aaron to make a golden calf for them to worship. They were extremely susceptible to the influence of the mixed multitude of non-Hebrews in their midst—to their censure, opinions and desires. In short, they were "carnal" (1 Cor. 3: 1, 2), living on a diet of milk, not yet of solid food.

In this picture, it is not difficult for us to recognize our own spiritual autobiography. But it was a necessary stage to prepare them for what God had in store.

THE KADESH-BARNEA CRISIS

When they reached the borders of the Land of Promise at Kadesh-barnea and saw its lush hills and valleys, one would naturally expect that in their eagerness to be the first to set foot on the sacred soil, the whole company would stampede. But no! they seemed as reluctant to enter Canaan as the majority of Christians are to embark on the spiritual experience of which it is the counterpart.

At God's command, Moses selected twelve spies to search Canaan and bring back their report—whether the people were few or many, strong or weak, and whether the land was good or bad (Num. 13:17-20). For forty days the spies searched the land and returned, laden with samples of its luscious fruit. There was full agreement that the land flowed with milk and honey, but there the agreement ended. The spies were divided into two groups. The majority report was presented by the Timorous Ten, the men of reason, and the minority report by the Trustful Two, the men of faith. And what startling contrasts the reports presented.

Ten: "We are not able . . ." (Num. 13:31).
Two: "We are well able . . ." (13:30).
Ten: "It is a land that eateth up the inhabitants" (13:32).
Two: "They are bread for us" (14:9).
Ten: "The cities are walled and very great" (13:8).
Two: "Their defence is departed from them" (14:9).
Ten: "We were as grasshoppers in their sight" (13:33).
Two: "Neither fear ye the people" (14:9).
Ten: "We be not able to go up against the people" (13:21).
Two: "Let us go up at once and possess it" (13:30).

The differing viewpoints can be explained by the fact that the majority looked at the strength of their enemy through the magnifying glass of unbelief. The minority gained a true perspective because they were men of faith.

The majority impeached *God's word,* as though He was a man who would lie. They impugned *God's power,* as though seven nations would tax His strength. They invalidated *God's goodness,* as though He was working for their destruction. Unbelief is not only short in memory, but defective in eyesight.

No sooner had the report been released than panic broke out among the people, for unbelief is unbelievably contagious. Instead of shouts of joyous anticipation, the voice of weeping rent the air the whole night long. They regretted ever leaving Egypt. "Would God we had died in Egypt or in this wilderness," they moaned. "Let us make a captain and return to Egypt" (14:24).

So stubborn were they in their refusal to enter the land, that only the appearance of the awe-full Shekinah glory in the midst of the Camp prevented them from stoning faithful Caleb and Joshua as they made one last moving appeal to the nation to trust in God.

The attitude of the ten spies has its modern parallel. There are always those who endeavor to discourage others from "going up to possess the land." They raise the bugbear of "sinless perfection." Because they have never experienced it, they assert that there is no such thing as a life of victory for the Christian. They argue that the Sermon on the Mount is not applicable today but is for a people living in a future age; the standards of that Sermon are too high for us here and now—forgetting that God has only one standard for the Christian, and that is Christ, the living embodiment of the Sermon on the Mount.

They press the truth that we received everything *in Christ* when we were converted so as to imply that we have it all *in experience,* ignoring the fact that it is available to us and will become ours only as we appropriate it.

They endeavor to frighten others away from any teaching about the Spirit-filled life, because some Christians have gone to extremes in their presentation of that subject.

They argue that sanctification is by elapse of time, growing in grace, instead of in response to faith and surrender to the Lordship of Christ (Acts 26:18). There is abundant evidence to prove that not every old person is "wholly sanctified," to use Paul's term.

A solemn responsibility lies on those who, like the spies, "bring a slander on the land" (14:36), simply because they themselves have "failed to enter in because of unbelief" or prejudice.

The legitimate wilderness experience of Israel lost its propriety from the moment they turned back in unbelief at Kadesh-barnea. From that point on, theirs was a sinful and rebellious experience. They *would not* enter in, and God ratified their decision by turning them back into the wilderness.

In their rebellion they said, "Wherefore hath the Lord brought us into this land to fall by the sword, that our wives and children, should be a prey?" (14:3). According to their fears it was to them. Because of their disobedience and unbelief, God pronounced a solemn sentence: "Your carcases shall fall in the wilderness, but your little ones which ye said would be a prey, them will I bring in, and they shall know the land which ye have despised" (14:29-33).

Of all that multitude of people, of those over twenty years of age only Caleb and Joshua, the men of faith, tasted the joys of Canaan. The remainder "fell in the wilderness," a silent testimony to the tragedy and sinfulness of unbelief.

Sooner or later in our Christian experience, we come to our own Kadesh-barnea crisis when we have to make a choice—will we press on to the Canaan-life or will we turn back to the unsatisfying and aimless life of the wilderness? It is well to keep before us the results of the latter course. Dr. C. I. Scofield has pointed out that these five things are involved in the illegitimate wilderness experience:

Restlessness. Israel had no settled homes. One day they were camped beside a beautiful oasis, next day they were traversing the scorching sands. The Christian living in the wilderness is harassed by anxiety and tormented with fears; restless in body and restless in mind. There are no *restful* Christians living in the wilderness.

Discontent. They were constantly murmuring against God and His chosen leaders. When God gave them bread from heaven, they craved flesh from Egypt, and forgetful of their cruel slavery, wished they could once again breathe its congenial atmosphere. The Christian living in the wilderness is preoccupied with his own troubles instead of fighting God's battles. There are no *contented* Christians living in the wilderness.

Fruitlessness. It is true that Israel fought and won battles in the wilderness, but it did not bring them any advantage, nor did they gain any territory. All they obtained was the right to pass through their enemy's territory. At the end of forty years of marching and fighting, they were as poor and landless as when they began. The battles of the wilderness Christian are battles of rebellion rather than of conquest. There are no *fruitful* Christians in the wilderness.

Negativity. Their main virtue was that they were not doing Egyptian things, although secretly they longed to do them. There was nothing positive, or aggressive about their lives. Many Christians who live in the wilderness do not drink or dance, smoke or swear, but having said that about them, you have said it all. Their lives are notable for the things they do not do. You look in vain for the aggressiveness of the spiritual warrior. There are no *positive* Christians in the wilderness.

Vacillation. The Hebrews alternated between the borders of Egypt and the borders of Canaan. When with worldly-minded people, the wilderness Christian would willingly join in their worldly pursuits, if it were not what others would say. Occasionally when away from home or observation by other Christians, he makes a secret excursion back into Egypt. Or at a special crusade or convention, he journeys to the Canaan border and longs to enter in, but always shrinks back at the thought of the cost. One day he enjoys communion with Christ, but the next doubts his salvation. There are no *stable* Christians in the wilderness.

If the above diagnosis matches the reader's spiritual condition, God has something far better than that.

The Spirit of God desires to allure from a disheartening life of carnality and self-pleasing to a life of victory and power. The choice is ours. We may, if we wish, turn back to the life of failure and longing and lusting of the wilderness, or we may press on into the Land of Promise. These words of warning from the Spirit are very explicit; and they are based on this very incident:

> Today if ye will hear His voice, harden not your hearts, as in the provocation, in the day of temptation in the wilderness: when your fathers tempted me . . . forty years. . . . So I sware in my wrath, they shall not enter into my rest. . . . Take heed, brethren, lest there be in any of you an evil heart of unbelief in departing from the living God (Heb. 3:7-12).

They had their last chance—and missed it! Their bodies fell in the wilderness. Never again did they have the opportunity of entering Canaan. We should fear to say, "Tomorrow," when the Holy Spirit says, "Today." The sad summary of their experience is given in the words, "So we see that they could not enter in because of unbelief" (Heb. 3:19).

> They came to the gates of Canaan,
>   But they never entered in;
> They came to the very threshold,
>   But they perished in their sin.
>
> And so we are ever coming
>   To the place where two ways part,
> One leads to the Land of Promise,
>   And one to a hardened heart.
>
> Oh! come in complete surrender,
>   Oh, turn from your doubt and sin;
> Pass on from Kadesh to Canaan,
>   And a crown and Kingdom win.
>
>   R. Kelso Carter

WHEN WE CANNOT SEE OUR WAY

When we cannot see our way,
Let us trust and still obey;
He who bids us forward go,
Cannot fail the way to show.

Tho' the sea be deep and wide,
Tho' a passage seem denied,
Fearless let us still proceed,
Since the Lord vouchsafes to lead.

Night with Him is never night,
Where He is, there all is light;
When He calls us, why delay?
They are happy who obey.

T. Kelly

12 POSSESSING OUR POSSESSIONS

Reading: Joshua 1

They came to the gates of Canaan,
But they never entered in;
They came to the very threshold,
But they perished in their sin.

THIRTY-EIGHT YEARS of aimless wandering in the wilderness had come to an end for the Hebrews since they turned back in unbelief at Kadesh-barnea. Once again in the providence of God the nation stood at the gate of the Promised Land. Their camp was pitched on the east side of the river Jordan, and they were ready to cross over into their long-promised inheritance.

But among the assembled company, only Joshua and Caleb remained of the adults of the generation who had turned back at Kadesh. All the others had fallen in the wilderness as God had said, a silent and solemn warning to all in this day who despise the spiritual counterpart of the earthly Canaan. Even Moses and Aaron who had spent their lives in sacrificial service for their nation were excluded from the Land, because they failed to honor God before the people—an important lesson to those in positions of spiritual leadership.

At this crisis in the history of the nation, God spoke to Joshua, "Moses my servant is dead; now therefore arise, go over this Jordan." What lies behind this rather strange sequence? What is the connection between the two clauses? An important spiritual lesson is symbolized here. Moses, whose very name is synonymous with the Law (which stands for man's best unaided endeavors), could never lead Israel into Canaan, even as man's best unaided efforts can never lead him into a life of rest, blessing and victory. Only our heavenly

135

Joshua, Jesus, can lead us there. The Canaan experience is not usually realized until, through the disillusioning experiences of the wilderness, we are brought to despair of attaining holiness through self-effort.

There is another lesson here, too. God's plans and purposes are not dependent on any one human instrument, however gifted and wise. He buries His workmen, but His work goes on unhindered by the change in personnel. Moses dies, but God has Joshua ready to assume leadership—one man, not the committee of seventy who had aided Moses in his administration.

When some outstanding human leader dies, it seems as though he can never be replaced, but time soon proves in a most humbling fashion that no man is indispensable to the purpose of God.

THE PROMISE OF POSSESSION

Israel had an unimpeachable title to the Land of Canaan. It became theirs by deed of gift. The memorandum of transfer is found in Genesis 15:18. God said to Abraham, "Unto thy seed have I given the land." The boundaries of the territory transferred are clearly stated, "from the river of Egypt to the great river, the river Euphrates."

The Divine Donor was fully entitled to make the gift, for in Genesis 14:18 He is revealed as "Possessor of heaven and earth." The Psalmist discloses the legal consideration for the transfer—"because I had a favour unto them," or in present-day legal phraseology, "in consideration of natural love and affection." No lawyer would dispute their title on legal grounds.

It should be noted that the promise was not, "I will give," but "I have given." It became legally theirs the moment God uttered the promise. They had legal title to it. But it became theirs in actuality only when they personally took possession of it. It is one thing to own property legally. It is quite another to enjoy it in personal possession.

For the Christian it is of the utmost importance to

realize that while many spiritual blessings are legally his by gift from God, he enjoys them in experience only when he personally appropriates them.

THE PREPARATION FOR POSSESSION

Consider the tremendous odds against which Israel must fight. Recent archaeological discoveries have demonstrated that the Hittites were a great and cultured people, sufficiently powerful to rival Assyria or Egypt. It was absurd presumption for this untrained horde of slaves to think they could dispossess and exterminate such highly organized nations as those which inhabited Canaan. There must be preparation before conquest.

Joshua himself must be prepared and encouraged before he was equipped for the conflict and conquest of Canaan. His preparation had both a divine and a human side.

On the divine side, there was the clear and specific call of God, accompanied by the *assurance of divine enduement.* "There shall not any man be able to stand before thee all the days of thy life" (1:5). Joshua must have felt utterly inadequate for the stupendous task he faced, especially as he was following in the steps of one of the greatest men in the history of the world. Despite inward trembling, calm assurance possessed him as the Almighty spoke this promise of a divine enduement adequate for the task, an enduement similar to that received by Moses at the beginning of his work.

Next, he was *assured of the Divine Presence:* "As I was with Moses, so I will be with thee" (1:5). It was in this promise that the secret of Joshua's indomitable courage lay. When God ordains our service, He also empowers it, and if we walk in step with Him, failure is impossible, for He is morally pledged to see us through. All His commands are enablings.

Again, there was *an affirmation of the Divine faithfulness.* "I will not fail thee, nor forsake thee" (1:5).

Strengthened by the presence of the God to whom nothing is impossible, and who had pledged Himself to see him through to the very end, Joshua would not find the prospect so formidable.

> Faith, mighty faith, the promise sees,
> And looks to God alone,
> Laughs at impossibilities
> And cries, "It shall be done!"

On the *human side,* Joshua was four times enjoined to be *strong and courageous.* "Be strong and of a good courage: for unto this people shalt thou divide for an inheritance the land" (1:6). Strength and courage were a *sine qua non* for a military leader about to engage in aggressive warfare. But the onus of being strong and courageous rested on Joshua, not on God. This was his responsibility.

Is it not a hollow mockery to tell a man conscious of his weakness and in the grip of fear not to be afraid? Is it not like telling a neurotic person not to worry? How could Joshua be strong and very courageous? Because he had the assurance of the presence of the mighty God with him, and He would neither fail nor forsake him. He must rest on God's plighted word. In spiritual warfare, courage that does not rest on the consciousness of God's presence and faithfulness, is presumption rather than courage.

Many of us, like King Uzziah, become *too strong* for God. Uzziah was "marvellously helped until he was strong, but when he was strong, his heart was lifted up to his own destruction" (2 Chron. 26:15, 16), and the mighty monarch became the loathesome leper. Joshua's courage was not self-generated, but derived from the realized presence of God. It was the product of conscious weakness plus constant dependence.

The very command, "Be strong," indicates that he felt weak, and "be not dismayed," that he was dismayed. It is reassuring that God has room in His army—even in the leadership of it—for those who are not strangers to these emotions, provided they draw on Him for strength and courage. It was as though God said to him, "Moses is dead, but I am not, so you can be strong and of good courage."

He was commanded *constantly to meditate on the Book of the Law,* God's written Word. "This book of the law shall not depart out of thy mouth; but thou shalt meditate therein day and night . . . for then thou shalt make thy way prosperous, and then thou shalt have good success" (1:8, 9).

The written Word of God was henceforth to be his handbook, his manual of instruction. Implicit obedience to it would constitute the secret of his success. This, not his sword, was Joshua's main equipment for victory. He must saturate himself in it, "day and night." There he would find his plan of campaign and his marching orders. If he neglected it, his courage would ooze out of his finger-tips when he came to meet his experienced foe.

Our tendency today is to immerse ourselves in a different type of literature, to spend an inordinate amount of time gazing at the TV screen and to leave little time for meditation in the Word of God. This is a fruitful cause of the weakness of the Church today. The recruit must master his weapons long before he reaches the front lines. Neglect of meditation—hard thinking, not dreamy reverie—results in an anemic spiritual life.

It is most instructive to note from a comparison of Ephesians 5:18ff. with Colossians 3:16ff., that the same results in Christian character and relationships follow from being filled with the Spirit as from being filled with the Word of God. The clear implication is that we will *remain* Spirit-filled only so long as we constantly meditate on the Word of God.

He was urged to *obey the Word of God in every detail*—"that thou mayest observe to do according to all the law (1:7, 9). This injunction is no less important than the previous two, for disobedience to light

139

received effectively prevents reception of further light. The Holy Spirit is given to those who *obey* Him." Disobedience leaves the devil in possession of a vantage ground from which he can carry on guerilla warfare in the soul.

On the part of the people, too, there must be preparation for crossing into the Land. "Prepare you victuals; for within three days ye shall pass over this Jordan, to go in to possess the Land" (Josh. 1:11). In three days the manna would cease, and the nation would have new fare to live on, the corn of the Land. The food that satisfied us for life in the wilderness will be inadequate to support spiritual life in the conquest of Canaan. For that we will require larger and more frequent food from the Word of God, a constantly expanding conception of our Great Commander, and a more intimate knowledge of His plan to campaign.

In the wilderness, Israel's food was prepared for them. Now that they were about to enter Canaan, they must learn to prepare their own. It is in this respect that the "carnal" Christian differs from the "spiritual" Christian. The former is dependent on human preachers and teachers to provide him with pre-digested food. The latter, even if shut away from all spiritual fellowship, will maintain his spiritual glow because he knows how to feed himself from the Word of God. The soldier on campaign carries his rations with him. A soldier who does not know how to look after his food and his feet will soon find himself out of active service. We must dig into the Scriptures every day, preferably the first thing in the day, and feed our souls on the great truths of Scripture — its warnings, reproofs and promises, and above all, on Christ Himself.

THE PRINCIPLES OF POSSESSION

In Joshua chapter 1, the principles on which Israel must possess the Land are either expressed or implied, and each has its counterpart in the experience of the Christian.

Dispossession

Before they could possess the cities and houses of Canaan, they must dispossess the present inhabitants. "And ye shall dispossess the inhabitants of the land and dwell therein" (Num. 33:53). Failure to dispossess them would inevitably bring discomfort and defeat. "If ye will not drive out the inhabitants of the land . . . they shall be pricks in your eyes, and thorns in your side, and shall vex you in the land" (Num. 33:55).

We have in embryo in our hearts the equivalent of the seven wicked nations of Canaan—pride, jealousy, impurity, dishonesty, covetousness, bad temper, unbelief and more besides. These must be dispossessed and driven out.

But is this not something we cannot do? Have we not tried and failed a hundred times? Perhaps these sins now seem more firmly entrenched than ever. The good news is that while we cannot, *God can and God will* as we trust Him. Here is His promise: "And the Lord said unto Moses, I will drive out the Canaanite, the Amorite, the Hittite . . . " (Ex. 33:24, 25).

> 'Twas most impossible of all
> That here in me sin's reign should cease,
> Yet shall it be! I know it shall!
> Jesus I trust Thy faithfulness;
> The thing impossible shall be,
> All things are possible to me.

Our part is to trust Him to fulfill His promise and drive out the spiritual enemies that have so often defeated us. Israel possessed only what they gained by dispossession.

Appropriation

The second principle was appropriation, one of the vital yet open secrets of the Christian life. Thousands of drab and defeated lives have been transformed simply through learning the art of appropriating, making our own, what God has given us. "Every place that

141

the sole of your foot shall tread upon, *that have I given unto you*" (1:3).

The whole land was given, but every square foot had to be personally possessed. The cities were already there, but the people must enter them. The houses were already built, but the Israelites must occupy them. They had to take possession of the land by walking over it foot by foot.

So it is with the broad land of God's promises. He has already given us every spiritual blessing: He ". . . *hath blessed us* with all spiritual blessings in heavenly places in Christ" (Eph. 1:3). ". . . his divine power *hath given unto us* all things that pertain unto life and godliness . . ." (2 Pet. 1:3).

There is nothing necessary for a life of holiness and victory which has not become ours by virtue of our union with Christ. But unless we plant the foot of faith on these blessings and claim them for our present experience, we are nothing the better.

William Penn from whom the State of Pennsylvania takes its name, so ingratiated himself with the Indians, that they made a gift to him of all the land he could walk around in a day. He rose early the next day and walked swiftly all day until dusk. When he returned to the camp, the Redskins quizzically said, "Paleface has had a very long walk today!" But they honored the trust he had placed in their promise. Surely we should not have less trust in our faithful God. When we claim one of His promised blessings, He will be as good as our faith. No amount of power or willingness in God can make up for lack of trust on our part.

The third principle is

Progression

They were not required to possess *the whole* land at once. "The Lord thy God will put out those nations before thee by little and little: thou mayest not consume them at once, lest the beasts of the field increase upon thee" (Deut. 7:22).

142

The promise was for possession one step at a time. Each day should see more territory in our lives brought under sway of our Master. And until the very end there will remain unexplored territory and unappropriated treasure. We are not expected overnight to attain the degree of holiness reached by a John Wesley or a George Muller. The crisis of sanctification leads into a never-ending process. We are to live holy lives in accordance with the light we have received.

THE PERILS OF POSSESSION

It was one of the tragedies of Israel's history, that even in the golden days of David and Solomon, much of the land still remained unpossessed.

There were two perils to which Israel succumbed:

Partial Possession

Joshua led them in many battles until the power of the nations of Canaan was effectually broken, but the records of the conquests were marred by the melancholy refrain:

"Nevertheless they did not drive them out."

"The children of Judah could not drive them out."

"The Canaanites would dwell in the land."

"There remaineth very much land to be possessed."

They made a disastrous mistake in allowing the nations to remain, through a failure of faith. We make a disastrous mistake in not asserting the authority over the sins and failures in our lives which God has given. Behind the assurance, "Sin shall not have dominion over you," lies all the power of the Risen Christ.

In the light of the magnitude of God's gift to Abraham's descendants, it is pathetic that they were content with the narrow bounds of Canaan, and not once did they fully conquer even that. Our spiritual charter, too, is much wider than our actual wealth. We receive pardon and rest and are content with that instead of pressing on to enjoy the privileges of sonship and joint-heirship with Christ. We revel in our justification, but fail

143

to press on to an experience of practical sanctification. We should not be content with partial possession of our spiritual inheritance.

Non-Possession

This was the second peril to which two and a half tribes succumbed. Reuben, Gad, and half of the tribe of Manasseh fell even further short of the divine ideal. They were content with only a brief excursion into Canaan, and then returned to the land they had selected for themselves on the other side of Jordan (1:12-15). They rested content just short of Canaan — near, but not in it. They pressed Moses to grant them the delectable pastoral land, and he acceded to their request.

Many Christians travel a long way toward Canaan. They come to the very borders of the Land, but the demands of absolute surrender and obedience are too stringent. Life and warfare in Canaan would involve too much renunciation and self-denial. Covered by the Blood of Christ, they have passed through the wilderness. They have even sampled the fruit of the Land. But they are not prepared to press right in. The temptation to settle just short of the Promised Land is subtle and strong, and many succumb to it and lose their full inheritance.

The history of these border-dwellers afford a serious warning to those facing the same temptation. They were the first of the tribes to fall before the invading Assyrians, and were swept into a captivity from which they never returned. God did not compel them to cross Jordan and enter the Land, but allowed them to have their own choice. Nor does He force His blessings on us. Rather, He ratifies our choice. It was written of Israel that, "He gave them their request, but sent leanness into their souls." Such is the experience of the border-dweller.

Then, too, they were a source of trouble to the nation ever after. They became like two separate nations, having different dialects and constant disagreements. A

144

border-dweller can always be detected by his dialect—he does not speak the "pure language of Canaan." It is a foreign language to him. Being "carnal," he will often be at variance with the outlook of the "spiritual" believer.

Who were the descendants of these people? The Gadarenes, who besought Christ to depart out of their territory! There is much in the history of these tribes to serve as a warning against being satisfied with less than crossing Jordan and entering the Promised Land.

THE JORDAN CROSSING

By Jordan's rushing stream I stand;
The rolling tide is deep and wide, I see no way;
I long to reach the Promised Land;
The desert life of inward strife I leave today;
    O Lord! from sin grant full release
    Give me Thy perfect peace.

The pillar sheds its glowing light
On corn and wine, on fields that shine in fairest dress;
But turns its cloud of darkest night,
To sighs and tears of weary years, my wilderness.
    With God behind, and God before,
    I'll reach the farther shore.

I look in vain for Moses' rod,
Yet on the brink I will not shrink, nor fear the tide;
Th' eternal word, the ark of God
Goes on before from shore to shore, the floods divide.
    I reckon I am dead to sin;
    God's word gives peace within.

I find the corn and wine and oil;
No Egypt's taste, no desert waste, no manna here;
I reap the richest of the spoil;
My feet now stand upon the land, no foes I fear.
    I trust in what my Joshua saith,
    And fight the fight of faith.

R. Kelso Carter

13 CLEAN OVER JORDAN

Reading: Joshua 3 to 4:16

THE CAMP OF ISRAEL had removed from Shittim and was now located on the banks of the river Jordan. The spies had returned with the reassuring news that the nations of Canaan were smitten with fear through hearing of God's interventions on Israel's behalf. Joshua had, in faith, accepted the victory God had promised, saying, "Truly God hath delivered into our hands all the land."

Then followed the crossing of the flooded Jordan, which is summarized under five phrases used in this passage of Scripture.

THIS SIDE JORDAN — *Counting the Cost*

"The land which Moses . . . gave you . . . *on this side Jordan*" (Josh. 1:15).

Though the Israelites were in sight of the Promised Land, a rushing torrent flowed between them and it. Before them lay difficulties sufficient to daunt the stoutest heart. God gave them a three-days' pause, apparently to enable them to realistically face the difficulties ahead.

Difficulties to face. The first of these was *Jordan's impassable flood,* for "Jordan overfloweth all its banks all the time of harvest" (Josh. 3:15).

The river, swollen by Mt. Hermon's melting snows, was swirling past their camp. Usually only a sluggish stream, it had now become a turbulent torrent. Could a more unsuitable time have been chosen to make a crossing? It was humanly impossible—just as impossible and hopeless as it seems to some who read these pages, that they should ever be delivered from the slavery of sin with which they have for years battled unsuccessfully. Like the Hebrews, we are shut up to God for deliverance.

The second difficulty was *Jericho's threatening embattlements* which could already be seen in the distance. "And the people passed over right against Jericho" (Josh. 3:16). Jericho with its white walls and verdant palm trees, was the key to Canaan. So strongly fortified as to be almost impregnable, the city guarded all the passes into the interior of the Land. Israel might well be forgiven if they were as fearful of what lay beyond, as they were of Jordan's rushing waters.

It is not difficult for us to envision our own threatening Jericho looming up in the distance, a Jericho that may be the strategic point of our whole Christian life. It may be public confession of Christ; an apology that should be made; a letter of reconciliation to be written; the terminating of some family feud; the relinquishing of long-cherished resentment; restitution which should be made or some neglected duty performed. Whatever it is, our Jericho must be vanquished if we are to know the peace and joy God desires us to experience.

Like Israel we face two alternatives, either cross the Jordan and face Jericho, or return to the illegitimate and frustrating wilderness experience.

Instructions to follow. The people were instructed to wait until they saw the priests bearing the ark of God before they left their tents. Between them and the ark was to be a distance of a thousand yards. Doubtless the purpose of this stipulation was that all should have a clear view of the ark.

They were now to enjoy a new experience of divine guidance. Hitherto they had been supernaturally guided by the cloud and fire. Now they were to be guided by the ark borne by their own countrymen. In the Promised Land, supernatural manifestation gives place to spiritual heart exercise. They were given no clue as to how they would cross the river. To them it was to be a matter of faith, not of sight.

148

The priests received only the instruction to take up the ark and pass over before the people. To Joshua alone did God reveal His plan of campaign.

Sanctification to accomplish. The command was, "Sanctify yourselves: for tomorrow the Lord will do wonders among you" (Josh. 3:5).

Here is enunciated an eternal spiritual principle—God's sovereign intervention awaits the discharge of our responsibility. We fix the time for the display of His power. God is not fitful or capricious. When we obey the law of the Spirit (Rom. 8:2), His infinite power is at our service. God's tomorrow of wonders depends on our today of sanctification. The windows of blessing are always bolted on man's side, not on God's. Our sanctification withdraws the restricting bolts and the showers are released.

If it be objected that sanctification is God's prerogative, it can be answered that there is also a very real sense in which we must sanctify ourselves. Paul expresses it in these words: ". . . let us cleanse ourselves from all filthiness of the flesh and spirit, perfecting holiness in the fear of God" (2 Cor. 7:1). This is something God cannot and will not do for us.

Our sanctifying of ourselves involves, negatively, putting away all that the Holy Spirit shows is alien to God's holy nature; and positively, the renewal of a complete surrender to Him and His service. When Israel sanctified themselves, they placed themselves without reservation at His disposal, and the wonders soon followed. It was not their sanctification alone that gained them the victory, but it was the essential human factor.

ON THE BRINK OF JORDAN — *The Step of Faith*

"When ye are come to *the brink of the water of Jordan* . . ." (Josh. 3:8).

When they reached the Red Sea, Israel found a path already made for them through its waters. All they had to do was to walk across. But not so at Jordan.

There was no evidence whatever to the senses that the way would open up before them. They had to "walk by faith, not by sight." As we advance in the Christian life, God weans us from dependence on sight and shuts us up to faith.

The white-robed band advanced until a space of a thousand yards lay between them and the people. Carrying the golden ark with its covering of blue, the priests reached the rushing waters and stood on the very brink of Jordan. It is not difficult to imagine the question arising in their minds, "What if nothing happens when we step into the flooded river?" But at the first touch of their feet, the muddy waters receded, and the way into Canaan was opened. God responded to their step of faith.

The secret of their triumphant crossing is hidden in the words: "Behold, the ark of the covenant of the Lord of all the earth passeth over before you into Jordan" (3:11). The ark was the visible sign of God's presence with His people, to lead them in triumph over their enemies. It was at every stage to be God's victory.

What the ark was to the Israelite, that and much more is what Christ is to us. When the feet of Jesus dipped into the river of death, its waters receded, so that we who are in Him can cross over on dry land. When He went down into death, He carried the whole Church in Himself into that death; but it is only as we claim personally our share in the benefits and blessings which His death and resurrection gained for us, that the Holy Spirit can make it actual in experience.

Between the Christian who aspires to a closer walk with God and the full Canaan experience, there always flows a Jordan which must be crossed. For Israel it was not a matter of *growing out* of the wilderness into Canaan, but of *going over* into Canaan. We do not automatically grow out of the wilderness experience any more than Israel grew out of the wilderness. It was the result of a decisive step of faith.

By Jordan's rushing stream I stand;
The rolling tide is deep and wide, I see no way;
I long to reach the Promised Land,
The desert life of inward strife I leave today;
Oh, Lord! from sin grant full release,
Give me Thy perfect peace.

IN THE MIDST OF JORDAN — *Buried With Christ*

"And the priests that bare the ark of the covenant of the Lord stood firm on dry ground *in the midst of Jordan,* and all the Israelites passed over on dry ground" (Josh. 3:17).

This symbolic action is replete with spiritual significance. The descent of the priests into Jordan finds its counterpart in these verses: "Are you ignorant of the fact that all of us who have been baptized into Christ Jesus were baptized into His death? We were buried therefore with Him by the baptism into death, so that just as Christ was raised from the dead . . . so we too might habitually live . . . in newness of life" (Rom. 6:3, 4, *Amplified*).

It is important to distinguish between the two complementary aspects of our Lord's death — substitution and identification.

The substitutionary aspect has in view deliverance from *the penalty and guilt of sin.* We are delivered from these by believing that on the cross Christ died *for* us, in our place. How do we know that this is the case? Because we feel it? No, but because God's Word reveals it, and we rest on what it says. We have no other source of knowledge of the significance of His death.

The identification aspect is concerned with deliverance from *the tyranny and dominion of sin.* We are delivered from these by believing that we were identified *with* Christ when He died on the cross. How do we know that we died with Christ? Because we feel it? No, but because the same Bible which tells us Christ died *for* us, assures us that we died *with* Christ. To be

151

consistent, if we believe one statement we must also believe the other to be true.

"Knowing this," wrote Paul, "that our old man is crucified *with* him, that the body of sin might be destroyed, that henceforth we should not serve sin" (Rom. 6:6).

When Christ died, this verse teaches, He did not die alone. Just as the whole human race was "in Adam" potentially in the Garden of Eden when he fell into sin, so the whole body of believers was "in Christ" when He died on the cross to atone for the sins of the world. All who are the natural descendants of Adam have received through him a sinful nature. So all who are the spiritual seed of Christ, receive the benefit of all that His death and resurrection secured. Our old unregenerate self was crucified with Him. It is for us to believe this divinely revealed fact, and to act on it as being true, for it is true.

This is not an *attainment* of certain advanced Christians, but a *fact* true of all believers. It was not a crisis which took place at some point in Paul's career through something he did. It is true of us, whether we believe it or not, and whether we derive any conscious benefit from it or not.

The reason for God's identifying our old self with Christ in His death is not far to seek. No house can have two masters. Our "old man" is incurably wicked and will never abdicate in favor of Christ, hence God must deal drastically with the usurper. He passed sentence of death on our old self, and that sentence was carried out at Calvary. And now to every Christian seeking deliverance from the power of sin, God says in effect, "Your old man, the traitor within, the cause of all your trouble, was nailed to Christ's cross. Count on this accomplished fact and act as if it were so."

How does this operate in actual experience? The exhortation is, "Even so consider [reckon] yourselves also dead to sin . . . but . . . alive to God . . . in

Christ Jesus" (Rom. 6:11, *Amplified*). It becomes actual in our experience in response to our considering [reckoning] it to be true, and in this we can have the aid of the Holy Spirit. ". . . but if *by the Spirit* you put to death the deeds of the body, you will live" (Rom. 8:13, RSV).

We cross Jordan in experience when we pronounce sentence on our old unregenerate selves, when we consent to die, when we hand him over to the Holy Spirit to execute the sentence of death in us. It is here that "reckoning" comes in. As I reckon, count on it as being really true—which it is—God will make my reckoning good.

To "reckon" is not to *imagine* something to be true which is really not true, but to *count* on something which is really true. It is not like a legal fiction, nor does it have anything to do with our feelings. It is a mathematical word meaning, "to compute"; "to calculate." It is an attitude of mind in which we count a thing to be true for reasons as sure as the mathematical law that two and two makes four. Spiritually, it means to count as true what the Bible says is true, whether we feel it or not.

Our reckoning does not make our identification with Christ a fact—it is that already—but it does enable us to realize its power and blessing. As we "reckon ourselves to be dead indeed unto sin," God will see to it that we will "no longer be in bondage to sin."

> I look in vain for Moses' rod,
> Yet on the brink I will not shrink, nor fear the tide;
> Th' eternal Word, the ark of God
> Goes on before from shore to shore, the floods divide,
> I reckon I am dead to sin,
> God's Word gives peace within.

But a dead man is not of much service to God or man. This is a purely negative though necessary aspect of truth. The priests did not remain in the midst of the river but came

"Command the priests that bear the ark of the testimony, that they come *up out of Jordan*" (Josh. 4:16).

When the nation had passed clean over Jordan, the command came to the priests to "come up out of Jordan." This, too, has its New Testament parallel. "For if we have been united with him in a death like his, we shall certainly be united with him in a resurrection like his" (Rom. 6:5, RSV).

Not only were we crucified and buried with Christ, but we were raised with Him too. It is significant that death is rarely mentioned in connection with the believer apart from resurrection.

How do we know that we were raised with Christ? Again, we simply accept in faith the sure Word of God, and count on it being true in our particular case. From Calvary there flows a dual stream—*a stream of death,* breaking the power of sin over us, and *a stream of life,* enabling us to walk in "newness of life."

> Risen with Christ, my glorious Head,
> Holiness now the pathway I tread,
> I am from bondage utterly freed,
> Reckoning self as dead indeed.

If it is objected that we have no consciousness of being either dead to sin or alive to God, the answer from Scripture is that at this moment *we are as much dead to sin and alive to God as we ever will be*. It is not that sin is dead to us, for it is as active and potent as ever, but as we reckon that we are dead to sin and alive to God, He will make both facts true in experience.

An act of the will

An act of the will is involved, not a mere reaction of the emotions. When Jesus confronted the man with the withered hand and commanded him to stretch it out, he might well have demurred, saying that he did not feel the power to stretch it out. But instead he reckoned on the Lord's good faith, and willed to stretch it out. God's enabling power came in between the act of willing and the act of stretching out his hand. If we act as if it were so, it will be so.

Abraham Lincoln's Emancipation Act which freed America's slaves affords a helpful illustration of this truth. The moment Lincoln signed his name to that historic document, every slave in the United States of America was *legally* free. No master had the power any longer to keep him in bondage. But every slave was not immediately liberated *experientially*. Before this took place several things had to happen—things which have their counterpart in the emancipation of the slave of sin.

1. The slave must *hear* the joyous news. Knowing, not feeling his legal freedom was the important thing.
2. Next he must *believe* the good news.
3. He must *reckon* on the news being true not only of slaves in general, but with respect to his own case in particular.
4. He must *refuse* any longer to be a slave, and *assert* his legal freedom from his former master.
5. In doing this he could *count on* all the power of the legislature of the United States of America being behind him as he refused further bond-service.

So with the believer. In His own blood Christ signed our Act of Emancipation. It is our part on hearing, to believe it, to count on it being true in our case, and to refuse to be longer ground under the heel of Satan and sin. In thus claiming our freedom, and saying, "No," to sin, we can count on all the power of the Risen Christ being behind us.

We need no longer continue powerless in service. Through our union with Christ in His resurrection we are "alive unto God," responsive to Him — alive to prayer, alive to calls to service, alive for testimony and soul-winning.

"All the people . . . passed *clean over Jordan*" (Josh. 3:17).

Immediately the priests came up out of Jordan, the waters rolled back, as cold and forbidding as ever, but all the people had passed clean over Jordan.

There was a *definiteness* about the whole incident. Jordan was the clear, definite boundary between the wilderness and Canaan. There was no need for them to ask, "Are we over Jordan?" We too will know when we have crossed Jordan.

There was *finality* about it. Between them and their old life of failure, lay Jordan's swirling flood. They had crossed their Rubicon and were shut in with their enemies. There was no possibility of retreat. Those who have entered upon Canaan-life, look back to see the river of Christ's death flowing between them and the old life of sin.

There was *newness* about it. For Israel, a totally new life had begun. There was *better food*. Manna was replaced by fruit, milk, honey, corn. There was a *better rest*. No longer were they aimlessly wandering in the desert, but they lived in their own homes. They had a *better song* on their lips and in their heart. They experienced *more victory* in their warfare. Such is the picture of the "walk in newness of life."

The Ark has gone before into the waters of Jordan, but we must follow by an act of faith. He of whom the Ark speaks can do for us as He did for Israel, and bring us, too, *clean over Jordan.*

> O sweet and blessed country,
> The home of God's elect!
> O sweet and blessed country
> That eager hearts expect!
> Jesus in mercy brings us
> To that dear land of rest,
> Who are with God the Father
> And Spirit ever blest.

WITHOUT A BLOW

I'm more than conq'ror through His blood,
    Jesus saves me now;
I rest beneath the shield of God,
    Jesus saves me now.
I go a kingdom to obtain,
I shall through Him the victory gain,
    Jesus saves me now.

Before the battle lines are spread,
    Jesus saves me now,
Before the boasting foe is dead,
    Jesus saves me now.
I win the fight though not begun,
I'll trust and shout, still marching on,
    Jesus saves me now.

I'll ask no more that I can see,
    Jesus saves me now,
His promise is enough for me,
    Jesus saves me now.
Though foes be strong and walls be high,
I'll shout, He gives the victory,
    Jesus saves me now.

Why should I ask a sign from God?
    Jesus saves me now,
Can I not trust the precious blood?
    Jesus saves me now.
Strong in His word, I meet the foe,
And, shouting, win without a blow,
    Jesus saves me now.

J. Parker

14 THE CONQUEST OF JERICHO

Reading: Joshua 5:13-15; 6:1-20

JOSHUA WAS FACING his second impossible situation. The first had been on the banks of the flooded Jordan river, this, before impregnable Jericho. The second seemed just as difficult and impossible as the first. Israel was confronting an entirely new situation. They had crossed their Rubicon, and had no fortresses to which they could retire. Retreat was cut off. All the old experienced warriors were dead, and the new troops were green and untried. True the Jordan was behind them, but Jericho lay ahead.

Joshua had received no special instructions from God as to the mode of attack he should adopt. Moses was dead and he had no one to consult. Small wonder that he decided to reconnoiter, and discover the strengths and weaknesses of the city. The very existence of the nation was at stake, for defeat would mean extermination. It was either conquer or die. The burden of leadership lay heavily on him and he must find some solution to the problem.

Let us recall what had happened. First the neglected rite of *circumcision was revived* at Gilgal (Josh. 5:1). Through their discontent and rebellion, Israel had become out of touch with God. All the years they had wandered in the wilderness they had neglected the sign of God's covenant with them, circumcision. This mark of their separation to God must be restored, the reproach of Egypt rolled away before God could unveil His plan. By their obedience, Israel had again taken their place as His covenant people.

Second, the *passover was again observed* (Josh. 5:10). This festival could not be observed by an un-

159

circumcised people. In the wilderness, Israel had neglected to observe this festive remembrance of their deliverance from Egypt. They had forgotten that they had been redeemed by blood. The remembrance and the observance must be renewed. The lesson for us is that Calvary must never be far from our thoughts, the cross must be central. It is not only the ground of our salvation, but the weapon of our conquest. Paul knew this. "I determined to know nothing among you save Jesus Christ and him crucified."

THE CONQUEST OF JOSHUA

As Joshua was examining the fortifications of Jericho, he had no idea that just where he was, he was going to face in a few moments the determining crisis of the campaign. Suddenly he found someone standing beside him. He had been self-absorbed, totally occupied with matters of military strategy. Now he saw a stranger standing, drawn sword in hand. Like a true military man, Joshua's hand flew to his sword while he challenged the stranger, "Art thou for us, or for our adversaries?" (Josh. 5:13). Are you friend or foe? "Nay," was the reply, "but as captain of the host of the Lord am I now come" (5:14). Neither enemy nor ally, but Commander.

Upon discovering that he was in the presence of the Lord of heaven, Joshua fell prostrate and worshiped. Then came the question which betokened absolute surrender, "What saith my lord unto his servant?"

But even prostration was not all that was required of him. "Loose thy shoe from off thy foot; for the place whereon thou standest is holy. And Joshua did so" (5:15). In the East, in approaching a person of eminent sanctity, it was a mark of reverence to cast off one's sandals. Only when Joshua had completely yielded himself thus, was God able to unfold His plan of campaign.

The revelation of God always brings us to our knees in contrition and reverence, and the vision comes when we look away from our petty preoccupations to the Lord of glory.

The Captain or Prince of the hosts of the Lord had come, not to supplement Joshua's leadership, but to supplant him as leader altogether. Not to help, but to control. Israel now had a new Supreme Commander.

When one is used to being in command, it is not always easy to be supplanted by another. But Joshua's concern was not with his own prestige, but the capture of Jericho. Had he refused to submit to the new Commander, he would still have had to face the impossible situation, but with only his own resources and abilities. He might study strategy and take lessons in scaling walls, he might use all his wit and energy, but he did not have what it took to gain the victory, and he knew it. So he accepted a complete transfer of authority, and henceforth the Prince of the hosts of the Lord dictated the strategy.

It was now the responsibility of the New Commander *to direct* both strategy and tactics. Joshua's part was to keep sensitively in touch with Him, and execute the orders.

It is of interest to notice in Scripture that when men accepted His sovereignty, the Lord became to them just what they needed at that particular time. To Abraham the pilgrim, God revealed Himself as a traveler; to the resistant Jacob, as a wrestler; to the soldier Joshua, as a warrior with a drawn sword. To the afflicted, God reveals Himself as the God of all comfort. God is always the complement of our present need.

The Prince had also a second responsibility—*to protect* His people. He came for the defense of Israel and for offense against their foes. He brought with Him *a third force,* a heavenly and unseen army, whose power would win the day. Had Joshua not surrendered, this third force could not have operated on his behalf.

The third responsibility of the new Commander was *to relieve* Joshua not only of the command but of all responsibility. It was no longer Joshua's lonely burden.

161

His act of surrender must issue in a continued confidence in His leadership. It is one thing to surrender to God in principle, and quite another to work it out in practice, and Joshua's surrender was soon put to the test.

UNORTHODOX STRATEGY

The strategy suggested by the new Commander was unorthodox, to say the least—contrary to both common sense and experience. Whoever heard of walking and shouting bringing down a vast city wall? There was no precedent for it. Then as now, every fresh step of faith we take leaves us open to a new test. But with the plan of campaign, the Commander gave assurance of victory, and on this Joshua planted both feet.

Joshua returned from his reconnaissance no longer a burdened man. Anxiety had vanished, and the shout of victory was on his lips. All things were now possible. Had Jericho already fallen that he was so assured? No, it was just as impregnable as ever, but that was no longer his responsibility. He had handed it over to Another and left it there.

There are several lessons of contemporary value that we can learn from this incident.

1. *Before Joshua could stand dauntless before his foe, he must stand devoutly before his God.* He had been pre-occupied with his own problems, inspecting the enemy's powerful defenses, every moment feeling the task to be more impossible. His eyes must be directed away from the impossible to God, with whom all things are possible. He came to reconnoiter the battlements of Jericho, but he had a personal encounter with God. We so easily become so pre-occupied with the problems, the forces opposing us, that God is obscured. Joshua had to learn that there was a spiritual side even to earthly warfare.

2. *Joshua had to surrender his command,* and pass the reins of authority into the hand of Another. He had to renounce his own strategy and tactics, except

162

as they coincided with those of his Commander. Henceforth the new Commander exercised absolute authority and had the right to demand implicit and unquestioning obedience, even if the reason was not immediately clear. On this personal crisis the whole campaign depended. The most significant moments in life are those when God reveals Himself. He had revealed Himself to His people in various capacities—as Redeemer, at the Passover; as Provider, in the manna; as Teacher, at Sinai; as Leader, in the wilderness. Now He reveals Himself as Commander of His people. "As Captain of the host of the Lord am I *now* come." God's self-revelation is progressive, and He is always revealing Himself in fresh ways. Each revelation is to meet a present need.

3. *Once he transferred the command, with it Joshua transferred the responsibility.* His part now was to obey. Up to this point everything depended on his own wisdom and skill, with the result that he was a deeply burdened man. After the crisis, he knew on whom to cast his burdens. Do we set the example of restful faith in our Master, or are we burdened with anxious care? Do we spread an atmosphere of faith and soundly-based optimism, constantly turning the eyes of others to our great God, or do we have about us an aura of pessimism? Are we confident of victory over our Jericho, or do we cherish only a wavering hope that fluctuates with changing circumstances?

4. *In public, Joshua was the leader,* and God supported and vindicated him in his leadership. But *in private he was the servant,* humbly seeking the plan of campaign drawn up by his Commander and carrying it out with meticulous care.

5. *Wherever there is a forbidding Jericho, there is a competent Commander,* if we will only lift up our eyes as Joshua did. We need never fight alone. There is a *third force,* a heavenly army which He will lead on to the field of battle. We are so terribly conscious

of the impregnability of our Jerichos, but how much greater is our Commander!

The conquest of Joshua was the essential prelude to

THE CONQUEST OF JERICHO

It would seem that Joshua drew up a plan of campaign which met with the approval of his Leader. His strategy was to drive a wedge into the center of the Land, west from Jerusalem, and thus split the opposition—the ancient plan of divide and conquer. He then planned to wheel south to eliminate the southern foe, and later mop up the remnant in the north. It is a striking tribute to his God-guided military genius that Allenby's successful conquest of Palestine in World War I was admittedly due to the fact that he followed Joshua's strategy.

Jericho with its white walls was the key to the land of Canaan. From it radiated all the roads and passes through the country. It was so strongly fortified as to be almost impregnable. So long as Jericho's walls held intact, the land was safe from invasion. Its capture was therefore a prime necessity.

It must be noted that the overthrow of Jericho was essentially *a conquest of faith,* not of arms. It was "by faith the walls of Jericho fell down after they were compassed about seven days" (Heb. 11:30). It was a venture involving a stupendous gamble on the faithfulness of God. The manna had ceased and the welfare state come to an end. The people had no homes in which to live. They had burned their bridges behind them. With Joshua's vital leadership, they staked all on the faithfulness of God. It was for them either victory or death.

It is to their credit that they stood up to the test of the new Commander's seemingly irrational plan of campaign. They might have been excused for questioning so quixotic a strategy, but their obedience was implicit.

"Now all these things . . . are written for our ad-

monition, upon whom the ends of the world are come,"
said Paul in First Corinthians 10:11. What can we in
our day, learn from this venture and victory of faith?
It involved:

The Obedience of Faith (Josh. 6:14). ⟺ faith ⇒ obedience

To march around the city once a day for six days
and seven times on the seventh day imposed a great
strain on the nation's loyalty and obedience. In this it
was Joshua, the earthly leader, who must take the
initiative. The people had never seen or heard the
authoritative commands of the Captain of the Lord's
hosts. Joshua must communicate his faith to the nation. This is one of the great functions of spiritual
leadership. No matter how inscrutable or imprudent
the divine commands might seem, it was for him to set
the example of unquestioning obedience. He must un-
hesitatingly count upon God's promise, although he
knew full well that from the human angle, the means
to be adopted were not adequate to the end. There
was little scope for originality or genius on his part,
but endless scope for faith and obedience.

It is noticeable both in Scripture and in Christian
experience, that God rarely interprets or justifies His
commands in advance, for this would rob faith of its
opportunity. The axiom of the faith life is, "What I
do thou knowest not now; but thou shalt know hereafter" (John 13:7).

The Discipline of Faith

"Ye shall not . . . make any noise with your voice,
neither shall any word proceed out of your mouth . . . .
so they did six days" (Josh. 6:10, 14).

What would be the most stringent test for a nation
notorious for complaining and criticising? Would it
not be the discipline of silence? It requires little
imagination to picture the confusion that would have
resulted if everyone were free to air his views on the
strategy that was being adopted. Unbridled criticism

and airing of doubts would soon paralyze the nerve of faith. They would have talked themselves out of faith before they completed the first circuit. There was and is great spiritual and psychological wisdom in muzzling the expression of unbelief.

It must have had a strange effect on the people of Jericho to watch this host of virile young men marching around the city in absolute silence, voicing no challenge, flinging no taunts, making no complaint. They could afford to be silent if they were inwardly relying on the promise of their omnipotent God.

They had also to exercise

The Patience of Faith

"So they did six days," and seven times on the seventh day (Josh. 6:14). This would be a tremendous test to young men itching to test their strength with that of the Canaanites. To do nothing but wait for God's time is much more difficult than taking the initiative ourselves.

As they neared the end of the thirteenth and final circuit, the walls of the city were as stout and forbidding as ever. There was not the slightest visual evidence that their collapse was imminent.

In the realm of answered prayer, this incident has much to teach us. Many of our prayers are not yet answered because we have not completed the thirteenth circuit of our personal Jericho.

"Unanswered yet? Nay, do not say ungranted,
    Perhaps your part is not yet fully done!"

Even on the completion of the thirteenth circuit the walls did not fall until they voiced

The Shout of Faith

"The people shouted with a great shout . . . the wall fell down flat, so that the people went up into the city . . ." (Josh. 6:20).

It is of the nature of faith that it believes and rejoices in advance of realization. Every step around

166

Jericho had been a step of appropriation by faith, but the climax came with the mighty shout of the people, the outward expression of inward confidence in their almighty God. It should be noted that the shout of faith arose while the walls were still intact. They shouted *before* the walls fell, not after. It would be easy to shout afterwards! Once again, in the second impossible situation they had risked everything on the faithfulness of God, and their faith received its reward.

A magnificent example of this shout of faith is given concerning Robert Moffat, father-in-law of David Livingstone. For several years Moffat had been engaged in missionary work among the people of Bechuanaland, but with no visible results.

One mail brought a letter from his church in Scotland, inquiring what they could send him as a Christmas present. In those days of slow mails, six months would elapse before he would receive their gift. As yet there was not a single convert, but in sublime faith, Moffat replied, "A communion service." This was his shout of faith in God. When in due course the communion service arrived, many new believers sat at the Lord's table with him as they used it for the first time.

> Before the battle lines are spread,
>   Jesus saves me now;
> Before the boasting foe is dead,
>   Jesus saves me now.
> I win the fight, though not begun,
> I'll trust and *shout* still marching on,
>   Jesus saves me now.

The Glorying of Faith

". . . all the silver, and gold, and vessels of brass and iron, are consecrated unto the Lord: they shall come into the treasury of the Lord" (Josh. 6:19).

In other words, all the glory was to be the Lord's. The victory was so obviously the sovereign work of God, that neither Joshua nor the people could take any glory to themselves.

The miracle of the conquest of Jericho achieved two

important objectives. It inspired Israel with confidence and enthusiasm as they faced the stupendous difficulties that lay ahead. It struck terror into the hearts of their Canaanite enemies and psychologically conditioned them for defeat.

It remains for us to face realistically our personal Jerichos and shout the shout of faith over them.

What is our forbidding Jericho? Is it the citadel of an unforsaken and unconfessed sin? Is it past failure? Is it an unanswered prayer? Is it a lost experience? Is it the Jericho of fear? Is it some domestic trouble? Whatever it is, face it, look away to your omnipotent and faithful Lord, and shout the shout of faith.

BE WATCHFUL

My soul, be on thy guard,
  Ten thousand foes arise;
The hosts of sin are pressing hard
  To draw thee from the skies.

Oh, watch, and fight, and pray;
  The battle ne'er give o'er;
Renew it boldly every day
  And help divine implore.

Ne'er think the victory won,
  Nor lay thine armour down.
The work of faith will not be done,
  Till thou obtain the crown.

George Heath

15 THE PERILS OF THE PROMISED LAND

Reading: Joshua 7 and 9

THE OUTSTANDING CHARACTERISTIC of life in the Promised Land, the Israelites soon discovered, was *conflict;* but conflict that issued in victory. They knew very little about fighting until confronted by the inhabitants of Canaan. They had been engaged in skirmishes with different groups in the Wilderness, but in Canaan conflict began in grim earnest and on a larger scale.

The Christian who imagines that life in the Promised Land of Christian experience is the end of conflict has a great disillusionment awaiting him, for there are not less, but more strong and subtle temptations than before. There is not less conflict but more constant conflict. The difference lies in the fact that in Canaan the battles are fought under the leadership of the Victorious Man with the drawn sword, who has never suffered defeat. It is not rest *from* conflict, but rest *in* conflict. In their first seven years in Canaan, Israel lost only one battle, and that was because of culpable sin and disobedience.

It should be borne in mind that Israel's warfare was not directed against the Canaanites merely as men, but against the Satanic powers to which they had yielded and whom they worshiped.

God had commanded the extermination of the Canaanites for two wise and sufficient reasons. First, they were *incorrigible demon-worshipers* in whose individual and communal life all the revolting and vile accompaniments of such worship were manifest. Secular history is sufficient to establish this fact without recourse to the divine record. For the sake of the human race they

171

must be cut off, lest all mankind be corrupted and drawn away into the same sins.

Second, they were *unspeakably immoral.* "Defile not ye yourselves in any of these things," God commanded His people, "for in all these things the nations are defiled which I cast out before you. *Therefore* do I visit the iniquity thereof upon it" (Lev. 18:24, 25). According to this passage, the extermination of the Canaanites was an act of *necessary moral surgery:* as beneficent an act in the interests of society, as is the excision of a cancer in the interests of the individual. God had taken up the nation of Israel to bless the whole of the human race. His purpose of blessing would have been thwarted had He allowed them to mingle and intermarry with the utterly corrupt and cruel Canaanites.

The Christian who has taken the step of faith and entered the Promised Land soon finds himself confronted with spiritual foes of which he knew little or nothing when living the carnal life of the Wilderness. Paul described them in these terms: "For we have to close in, grapple not with human flesh and blood alone, but with principalities, with powers, with the lords of darkness whose present sway is world-wide, with the spirit-host of wicked beings that haunt the upper air. Therefore take up the God-given panoply" (Eph. 6: 12, 13, Way).

Using Old Testament symbolism to illustrate New Testament truth, in Egypt, in type, the conflict is with *the world.* In the wilderness against Amalek, the conflict is with *the flesh.* In Canaan against the seven nations, the conflict is with *the devil and his hosts,* who resist our entrance into the heavenlies in Christian experience, and threaten to arrest our progress in the spiritual life.

THE INITIAL REVERSE — *At Ai* (Josh. 7)

There is much to learn from this, the only reverse which Israel suffered in its seven-year occupation of Canaan. The outstanding lesson is to *beware of pre-*

sumption. The fact that this defeat came close on the heels of the magnificent conquest of Jericho, invests it with deep significance for the believer who has only recently become a resident of Canaan.

Not long before, they had crossed the Jordan and were filled with optimism because God had promised them the victory. They expected Him to put their enemies to flight and give them the Land of Promise. They had crossed the flooded Jordan in safety, only to face impregnable Jericho. But as they obeyed their great Commander and shouted the shout of faith, the walls of Jericho had fallen.

Now, fresh from that exhilarating success, they had sent a small contingent to attack the small city of Ai. They had expected an easy victory over an insignificant enemy, but at the close of the day, Joshua and the leaders of Israel were prone upon the earth, with dust on their heads and their clothes rent. Israel had turned their backs upon their enemies. Thirty-six of their soldiers lay dead. It seemed that in spite of His promises God had forsaken them. And what were these promises when compared with the indisputable logic of facts?

One defeat would lead to another. Their enemies would hear of it and regain confidence. They would surround them and cut them off. In his bewilderment and distress Joshua's faith staggers and he cries, "Alas, O Lord God, wherefore hast thou at all brought this people over Jordan, to deliver us into the hands of the Amorites, to destroy us? would to God we had been content, and dwelt on the other side Jordan" (Josh. 7:7). What could Joshua say, after he had boasted to his people of what God had promised? "Oh, Lord, what shall I say?" was his agonized enquiry.

To his question the Lord answered in effect, "Why have you fallen on your face? Get up. You speak as if it were I who was to act. It is not I, it is you. Get up. Sanctify the people. Israel has sinned. Search out the sin and deal with it. So long as you neglect to do

173

this, you will not be able to stand against your enemies. I will not be with you any more unless you destroy the devoted thing among you." Humiliation and prayer is good in its place, but it is no substitute for judging sin.

Although Ai was small and apparently insignificant, it was in reality second only to Jericho in its strategic importance. It dominated the road to Jerusalem and guarded most of the passes into the interior of Canaan, and was therefore far from being as unimportant as it seemed. Israel learned at Ai, as we may learn if we do not heed the lesson, that *defeat is possible in the Promised Land*—possible, but not inevitable.

Causes of Defeat

First there was *presumption,* engendered by their resounding success at Jericho. They acted as though theirs had been a victory of arms at Jericho, instead of a victory of faith. The lesson for us is that the hour when flushed with recent victory and success is an hour of great danger. We may not rest on past victories. Each new battle, whether large or small, is a fresh challenge to faith and dependence on God. Success in public may well be followed by humiliating defeat in private, through this same sin of presumption.

Second, there was *underestimation of the foe.* Acting in carnal wisdom, instead of seeking their strategy from their Commander, they elected to send spies ahead to discover the strength of the enemy and determine the method of attack. Hearing that the people of Ai were few, they decided to send only a small contingent instead of the whole of the people.

Their experience should teach us that there is no sin so small that we can defeat it ourselves, no situation so simple that we can resolve it without divine help.

Then, *Joshua,* the divinely ordained human leader, instead of leading the army, *remained in the camp.* His place was at the head of his people, for it was his responsibility to interpret to them the strategy of the heavenly Commander.

Prayerlessness was another contributory factor in the defeat. It was not that Joshua did not pray, but he prayed at the wrong time. Had he prayed *before* the attack instead of *after,* they would have known no defeat. Had they made the same preparations before Ai as before Jericho, how different the story would have been. The Unseen Commander would soon have revealed to Joshua the guilty mound in Achan's tent. Defeat came because he left God out of his calculations.

The Nature of the Sin

Before the assault on Jericho, the people of Israel had solemnly devoted to God all that they would find in Jericho. The silver, the gold, all the possessions of the people of Jericho were to be holy to the Lord and were to be placed in His treasury. Joshua warned them of the seriousness of the sin of taking what had been devoted to the Lord for themselves in words that were crystal clear: "And ye, in any wise keep yourselves from the accursed thing, lest ye make yourselves accursed, when ye take of the accursed thing, and make the camp of Israel a curse, and trouble it" (Josh. 6:18).

Achan had joined with his fellow-Israelites in devoting to God the spoil of Jericho, but when he entered the city and saw a Babylonish garment, the silver and the wedge of gold, he coveted them. He knew they were God's, but he wanted them for himself. So he took them and hid them in his tent, and by this act he brought ignominious defeat to the whole nation.

It was a *small sin,* or at least it seemed so. Achan took only a very small part of all the spoils of Jericho. But judged by its effects on him and on the nation, it was by no means small. Indeed there is no such thing as a small sin. ⟹ small sin is not small

It was a *secret sin.* No one knew about it. He thought it was locked up in his own heart, but before long it was common knowledge to the whole nation. Secret sin has public consequences. There was no outward and obvious connection between Achan's sin and

175

The thirty-six corpses outside Ai, and yet they were intimately connected. The demoralization of the whole nation surely could not be attributable to some clothing and some gold and silver. And yet that was its cause.

His was *willful sin* for he had received due warning of its seriousness and consequences.

His *sin involved others*. He sinned not only against God and others, but against his own family and nation. He brought dishonor on God's name, shame, death and suffering to his nation and family, and the judgment of God on himself. We can never sin in isolation. The sin of the father affects wife and children. The sin of the church member affects the church. Our relationships are so intertwined that our failure influences the other lives around us. One drop of poison injected into the little finger will kill every member of the body.

Achan's was a sin *in the devoted thing*. He took something he had no right to have. The Babylonish garment should have been destroyed and the gold and silver placed in the treasury of the Lord. There may be things in our homes that have no right to be there. There may be money in our bank account which ought to be in the Lord's treasury and it is because of this that we are experiencing spiritual defeat. It is for us to judge the sin and put things right.

It is of more than passing interest to notice that the word used in the Septuagint Version of Joshua to describe Achan's sin, is the same word as is used in Acts 5:1, 2 to describe the sin of Ananias and Sapphira. They, too, took for themselves a portion of what they had devoted to God, and their sin brought on them the judgment of God. We too can keep back part of ourselves—our time, talents, and possessions, while professing to give all. We sing—

> Were the whole realm of nature mine,
>   That were a present far too small;
> Love so amazing, so divine,
>   Demands my soul, my life, my all.

But we do not always live up to the implications of our singing. All that we are and have, are His gifts, a trust to be used for His glory and to be always at His disposal. Achan confessed his sin—"I have sinned against the Lord." Have we?

CORRECTION OF THE DEFEAT

We can thank God that there is no defeat we may suffer for which there is not forgiveness, restoration and subsequent victory. The way in which Israel recovered from its initial reverse is most instructive.

Joshua was obedient to the message from God and placed himself once again under the direction of the Unseen Commander whom he had temporarily ignored. God was once again at the head of His people, and was able to work for them. He followed the heavenly strategy by acting contrary to the advice of the spies, and sending the whole host up against Ai. He searched out and judged the sin which had been the cause of the national defeat. The offender was singled out and charged with his sin. In four vivid verbs he told the tragic story: "I saw . . . I coveted . . . I took . . . I hid," four verbs which have spelled the doom of many another since Achan.

There are varying views of the punishment which was meted out for this sin, as the verse recording the event is capable of more than one interpretation. It reads, "And all Israel stoned *him* with stones, and burned *them* with fire, after they had stoned *them* with stones. And they raised over *him* a great heap of stones . . ." (Josh. 7:25, 26).

There is no doubt of the stoning of Achan, but were his wife and family also stoned and burned with fire? Dr. Alfred Edersheim, the great Hebrew Christian scholar, maintains that it does not necessarily follow that his sons and daughters were stoned and burned with him. In this case, the plural "them" could refer to only the oxen, asses, sheep and all that Achan possessed (v. 24). The record does not say that his wife

177

and family were implicated in his sin, or even *that they knew* of it, and this would favor the interpretation suggested above.

The tragedy of Achan is that had he waited only a few days, he would have had far more than the things he purloined, for Israel was permitted to take all the spoil of Ai. Endeavoring to snatch blessings before God's time has arrived can end in tragedy.

THE INITIAL COMPROMISE — *With the Gibeonites* (Josh. 9)

If the central lesson of the defeat at Ai is to beware of presumption, the lesson of Israel's involvement with the Gibeonites is, *Beware of snares.*

Once again Israel is flushed with success after the rout of the men of Ai. With the onward victorious march of the invaders, however, the surrounding nations proclaimed a truce in their inter-tribal warfare, and united against the common foe.

The Gibeonites (who were Hivites) however, were doubtful as to the wisdom of fighting against Israel, and they decided to adopt the strategy of deception. They sent ambassadors of peace who professed to have come from a distant country. Their appearance corroborated their story—old sacks, old wine-bottles, old shoes, tattered garments, moldy bread. The Israelites were suspicious at first, but the visual evidence was so convincing. It was here that they made a fatal blunder. "And the men took of their victuals, and asked not counsel at the mouth of the Lord" (v. 14).

Satan is far more dangerous in his wiles than in his overt assaults. The early Church flourished under the persecutions of Nero, but succumbed to the flatteries of Constantine.

In this case, the story was so plausible, the Gibeonites' allusions to Jehovah so reverent, their appearance so consistent with their claims, that the Israelites accepted the circumstantial evidence, and "asked not counsel at the mouth of the Lord." They trusted their own discernment and good judgment, a mistake so often perpetuated by the followers of Christ. We should never place final trust in our own judgment, however well balanced we consider it to be. The decision of the lower court of our judgment should be checked in the higher tribunal of God's Word. We can never afford to neglect seeking counsel of God, for we are no match for the subtlety and cunning of our enemy.

When our common sense is most sure of a course of action, it is wisdom to make doubly sure by consulting the Unseen Commander who is aware of the snares and wiles of the devil which may be hidden from us.

Joshua had not mastered the lesson of the failure at Ai. He was too hasty to wait on God. His suspicions were lulled by appearances. He made the mistake of "judging by the sight of his eyes and the hearing of his ears" (Isa. 11:3). In time of battle we should suspect everything and be on the alert to detect the devil's snares.

To his utter dismay, Joshua learned in three days' time that these citizens from a far country were his next door neighbors! But the discovery came too late. He had made a compact with them, and God would not allow the Israelites to break their plighted word.

In the years that followed, the divine prediction was fulfilled, for the Gibeonites were a burden to Joshua and a curse to Israel. Compromise with evil always brings trouble and discomfort.

God, in His gracious dealings with His erring people, overruled their failure and brought blessing out of the curse. The Gibeonites became "hewers of wood and drawers of water" to Israel, hewing wood for the burnt-offering, and drawing water for the cleansing rites and drink offerings, as well as for more mundane purposes. The Israelites were thus liberated from these menial tasks to prosecute the warfare against the seven nations of Canaan.

God frequently allows the results of our compromise to run their natural course, but at the same time He

179

makes them serve our spiritual development and eternal welfare.

The lesson from the compromise with the Gibeonites is, *Beware of snares*, beware of appearances, watch as well as pray. 凡事藉着禱告......

Such are some of the representative perils Israel met in the Land of Promise, from which the alert Christian can profit greatly. Although many victories were achieved, God's ideal for the nation was never fully realized. The writer of the letter to the Hebrews makes this clear in his comment on the nation's experience under Joshua's leadership:

"For if Jesus had given them rest, then would he not afterwards have spoken of another day. There remaineth therefore a rest to the people of God" (Heb. 4:8, 9).

Israel perpetually fell just short of God's full purpose for them. Never once did they possess *all* the land He had given. Never once was the year of Jubilee (with its implications of absolute surrender to the sovereignty of their God and correct relations with their fellow-men) really observed. The "rest" they experienced in the land was always temporary. The true rest, "the rest of faith," awaited the advent of the heavenly Joshua who alone was able to say, "Come unto me and I will give you rest."

The rest of God is no longer relegated to the future, but can, in response to our faith, be entered upon and enjoyed here and now.

> "We which have believed *do enter into rest.*
> . . . Let us therefore fear, lest, a promise
> being left us of entering into his rest, any
> of you should seem to come short of it."
>
> Hebrews 4:3, 1

> My Saviour, Thou hast offered rest,
>   O give it then to me!
> The rest of ceasing from myself,
>   To find my all in Thee.